The 52

DISCOVERING THE TRUE YOU
IN 52 SIMPLE LESSONS

by Deanne Mincer

Inspired By the Profound Teachings of
A Course in Miracles,
Classic Yoga Texts,
and the Mystical Poetry of Rumi

ISBN: 0692293264
ISBN 13: 9780692293263
Library of Congress Control Number: 2014916838
Light of Eternal Love Productions, Ridgefield, CT

www.deannemincer.com

Author's notes and Disclaimer

The teachings and lessons in this book were derived from many
sources and through the author's personal experiences. The stories
that are a part of the material reflect the author's remembrance of
certain events. While many life change suggestions are made, the
author, publisher, and distributor disclaim any responsibility from
the use of this information or concepts within this book.

TABLE OF CONTENTS

DEDICATION

To my husband, Richard, for his loving and unceasing support
in all my efforts, spiritual and otherwise.

To my mother, Esther, for showing me unconditional love
while in her body, and for teaching me the meaning
and depth of eternal love afterward.

To my many spiritual teachers, both alive and in spirit,
who guided me throughout this process.

INTRODUCTION

52 weeks. 52 lessons. 52 sparks for discovering who you really are. By this time, next year, you could be a whole new you. More light and happy. More joyous and peaceful. More at home in the world. More able to recognize that you, (yes, you) are a being of Divine and Eternal Love. You could find yourself transformed and at ease. Made over, in effect, yet, with feelings of love and compassion for the person you "used" to be. You will have discovered the True You.

We know that lasting change seldom occurs overnight. If too much is expected, most of us are destined to become frustrated. We just give up. It is easy to make resolutions that are far too ambitious at the new year or anytime we feel so motivated. So we will take this one lesson, one week at a time. I suggest you be gentle and patient with yourself. Let change unfold in natural ways. Little by little, week by week, see how you feel. If you skip a lesson or decide it's not resonating with you, just keep reading the weekly lessons and see which ones seem just right for you at the moment. You will know!

Of course, it won't take a year for you to notice that you are changing. It begins the minute you decide to start. Right now! But, take this as a special warning—whatever happens, this program and these lessons do not have any space for guilt or self-judgment. It is not designed to harp at you or castigate you. It is here to offer gentle and nurturing ideas that are easy to embrace in short periods of time. You will see that there will be an array of choices and types of ideas that you can choose to implement on your own. Even choosing a few and then following them continually, yet easily, will afford tangible results.

What you will read here is the result of what I see to be the synchronicity of many spiritual roads, all meeting in one place—in the presence of Divine and Eternal Love. I have spent more than twenty five years as a teacher of yoga and spiritual insights, working with scores of students who wished to feel happier, stronger, better able to cope with their lives and more willing to love themselves. *The 52* emanates from extensive study of *A Course in Miracles,* reading every word many times over and running "Into the Light of Miracles," Study Groups for *A Course in Miracles.* Inspiration also came from a totally unexpected mystical encounter I had with the Sufi poet/saint, Rumi, while visiting his shrine in Konya, Turkey, and thereafter embracing the Truth of his writings. We might call this a summary of my teachings or, as one person called it (though I laughed when I heard it)–the "Deanne Sutras."

My writing is very personal. I have been where you have been— discouraged, afraid, disheartened, depressed, and grieving. Alternatively, I have lots of experience with these—joyous, happy, hopeful, and full of love. We humans are all the same in this regard. At the core of our being, we search for the same things. I have been blessed to meet certain gifted teachers and guides. I have read and understand spiritual texts spanning yoga, *A Course in Miracles,* Christianity, Buddhism, the Sufi branch of Islam, and Judaic writings. Somehow, the wisdom in those writings merged into one simple understanding about Divine Love from that Source of Divine Love.

Each week I will offer tangible methods you can employ in your daily life. They may engage thoughts and affirmations, breathing methods and body movement, or using your senses to experience the world differently. They will be easy, I promise, yet they will emanate from profound spiritual teachings. Some lessons, by design, will be shorter than others. There will be variety in pacing. And I will want to know what you think and how you feel. You can contact me through social media or my website, www.deannemincer.com. We will share and guide and teach each other. We will see a Oneness in ourselves as the perceived differences fade and duality disappears. All of this process will be bathed in love, gratitude, and acceptance.

You see, I already KNOW who you are. It is not a secret to me, even if it is for you at this time. You are nothing less than the Light of Divine and Eternal Love. In the course of these studies and the days ahead, it is my fervent hope that you will come to know this for yourself.

You are on the road to knowing who you are, have always been and will be into eternity. Let's start walking...

Lesson 1

LOVING YOURSELF

Here we go! This is a lesson on love, my favorite topic. Try this: say to yourself, "I love myself completely NOW." Say it on the hour. Say it before sleep and on rising. Say it when the phone rings or the dog barks. Say it when someone says something upsetting or when you do something you wish you hadn't. Find a cue to remember those words. Write it down and put it on a sticky note where you can see it. No one else needs to see it. Say it even if you are saying it by rote. Even if you find it hard to believe. Just keep saying it–like a mantra.

This lesson on love is one of the most popular topics in my classes. I always tell my students about one of my best friends, a kindred spiritual sister and artist, who told me this story:

She was teaching a special children's art class at the ashram (a spiritual monastery) where she lived. Her guru (spiritual teacher) requested that she take on this task of teaching the children. As the class ended and the children's parents arrived, it was my friend's responsibility to inform them of what had been taught in the class. When she began to speak to them, only gobbledygook came out of her mouth. Try as she might, she could make no sense. They stared at her in amazement. She grew embarrassed and then felt like a fool. To make matters worse, she felt that she had disappointed everyone, especially her guru. After everyone left she sat in meditation, looking, praying to know why this humiliation had happened and what to do about it. Then the answer came! She was given explicit directions. She was told to take out a sheet of paper and write and say, "I love myself completely now," over and over again until she knew it to be true. Until the pain and humiliation subsided and until she remembered that there was NEVER a reason to do anything but love herself completely.

Everything happens with purpose.

Now, you can do this. Even when you are ashamed or lost or fearful. Let the words sink into your heart. The love will move through you and around you. You will call forth potent powers of love to surround you. But you must say it, silently or out loud, all week long.

In *Believe in Love,* Swami Gurumayi Chidvilasananda said:

The great devotional scriptures of India teach us that to cultivate and purify our experience of love is a sadhana, a genuine spiritual path. On this path, the means is love and the goal, again, is love.

I love myself completely NOW! Say it and see what happens. When you KNOW that it is true and nothing will ever change this, a spark of light will be ignited within you. The Light of Divine Love.

Lesson 2

HOW CALM AND RELAXED
ARE YOU RIGHT NOW?

"The body is the temple of the spirit."
—Amrit Dasai

It's time to scan your body. That's right. It's the body that seems to contain your Eternal and Divine Spirit. Just how light, happy, and full of love can you be if your body is tight with anxiety, like a twisted knot? It is important to take every part of our being into account on this joyous ride of Love. We don't overlook any aspect of ourselves, including our physical presence.

LOVING AND NURTURING YOUR BODY

This is the focus of Lesson Two—getting to know when and how your body reacts to stress. Tense muscles. Tight jaw line. Scrunched shoulders. The back held in a noose. Do you recognize these stress symptoms? Some bodies choose to display stress in one or two or all of these ways at once. Then most of us walk around all day long, unconscious and never noticing. But, once you know, you can start eliminating the body's reaction to stress and negativity. You can have a new dialogue with your body, while being compassionate and kind all the while. You can learn to love your body as another expression of your being.

Here is what to do: talk soothingly to your body, reassuring it and sending it love. "Go ahead, shoulders, take a little break. Soften up," you might say, or "There you go, you tense back, how about a little rest right now? Stretch out. Doesn't that feel good?" It's your body, after all. You can have a friendly chat with it. You might not want to do it out loud if you are in a public place, but then people will maybe just think you are talking on your cell phone. Or that you are a little odd. No matter!

I used to work in a place that was vibrating with tension. Executive decisions were made, and then rescinded all the time. It was the land of the ten-minute decision—in ten minutes there would be another, conflicting decision. The stress was palpable and everyone worked in close contact, seated in the same area. The only retreat was a bathroom stall. I would go in there and stand for a minute or two and imagine a flow of soothing warm water pouring over my body, washing away tension. I imagined the stress dripping off of my fingers and pooling at my feet, then flowing away. It worked, even in a bathroom stall. If it could happen there, it could happen anywhere. But that was then. Now I don't need to go anywhere; I can do the scan and the imagery where ever I might be. You can too, once you are used to the idea.

Remember your body reacts to what you think about it and say to it. It knows when you are sending it nurturing and love. You can love ALL parts of your being at once. Try some of these ideas:

- Honestly scan your body and be aware of tightness and stress. Consciously give it permission to let it go.

- Repeat this scan often throughout the day and even at night in bed, if you are awake enough to notice.
- You will see that your body reacts to these changes. Each time it will be easier to calm the body.
- Think of any parts of your body that have been problematic or are sensitive to negative thoughts. You may not like certain parts of your body or the way the body looks. Actively send kindness and love to these places in particular.
- Imagine Love and Light massaging and filling those parts of your body. Perhaps inhaling Love and Light and then exhaling away judgment, pain, and anything negative lodged in those spots.
- Take a class in deep rest and meditation. I teach Yoga Nidra (sleeping meditation), and it works so well at deflating stress, and can also take you to a level of consciousness where you surpass the body and only Love exists. "Divine Love: A Unique Yoga Nidra Experience," made in concert with Sacred Acoustics, is now available as a CD. It is designed to bring deep calm and elevated consciousness.
- See your body, from which you will surely part one day, as another expression of Divine Consciousness, of God. Treat it with tenderness and respect while you have it.
- Say these words over and over until they ring in your mind—I love my body and myself completely NOW.

I am honored to join you in learning to love yourself more. It is the true purpose in living.

Lesson 3

WHAT'S THE USE
OF WORRYING?

Do you think that worrying is a modern-day problem? Here is what Ovid, born in 43 B.C. and a Roman poet, had to say:

> *"Happy is the man who has broken*
> *the chains which hurt the mind,*
> *and has given up worrying once and for all."*

Can you imagine giving up worrying once and for all? Especially now, in a world where we seem to dwell on subjects like these: the undulating economy; terrorism and shootings; countries at war. Will we have enough money to put our children through college? Enough money to support us into old age? Enough money to buy food for tomorrow? What is our future? Can we find a job? Is the planet over heating? Why am I so depressed? On and on, more and more...

STOP! Has your worrying level gone up just by reading these questions? STOP! Put them in the box or slot them into worry time. Worrying about all this is useless, non-productive and dangerous. STOP NOW!

LET GO OF WORRYING

I like what William James, the psychologist/philosopher, had to say about worrying:

"If you believe that feeling bad or worrying long enough will change a past or future event, then you are residing on another planet with a different reality system."

•

I think, at least for now, we all seem to be on the same planet. The facts are in—worrying is wasted. It is time to break the habit! While loving yourself completely NOW and calming your body, you take the next step and stop worrying. Let it go. Give it up. Trust in Supreme Consciousness. All this worrying stuff is *out there* in another realm some of us call *maya* (illusion). But more on that later. Right now we are just being practical.

There is a song from World War I titled, "Pack up Your Troubles in an Old Kitbag and Smile, Smile, Smile." It goes on to ask us "what's the use of worrying?" and advises that "it never was worthwhile." You may think these lines are simplistic, but they fall on the truth. You CAN pack up your troubles and learn to place them in a healthier context. And smile, smile, smile.

Here's an idea I got from a friend and wonderful meditation teacher. Put one of those stretchy bracelets on your arm. Whenever you have a worry thought, switch it to the other arm. Or take some object, place it on your left then move it to your right whenever a worry erupts. You will quickly become aware of how often you worry. You might be moving it back and forth all day long. Count this as a bonus. At least you will know what you are thinking. In fact, you can try this with any number of thought patterns. First you have to be made aware of your worrying habits.

Here are some suggestions you might try:

- Become aware of your worry patterns. Use the idea just suggested or just mentally note whenever you have a worry thought. Don't be harsh with your self. This is not a reason to feel guilt. You are simply observing and learning.
- Put your worries in your "worry box." Each time you note a worry thought, rather than immediately obsess about it and create anxiety, write it down on a piece of paper and put it, literally, in a box. Then, when you are ready to address your worries, pull it out along with the others you have accumulated, and go ahead, worry. Limit the time you give to this. Worry away!
- Schedule a specific "worry time." Take your worries, as they arise, and note them in your mind, but do not spend any time on them. Then, at your chosen time— maybe on the hour of the clock and for two minutes— go ahead and worry like crazy. With wild abandon, worry. When the "timer" goes off, put them away again. Or choose one or two times a day when you will worry. Keep it contained so worrying is not running amuck throughout your day.
- Honestly evaluate what the worrying has done for you and to you. It won't take long before you realize that it is wasted effort.
- Do not mistake worrying for problem solving. They are two different things. One has a concrete outcome, the other does not.
- Throughout this process, remember that you can always return to your affirmation, I love myself completely NOW. Let it remind you that worrying (and nothing else) will ever take that love away. It emanates from a source far too powerful to be set aside by our behaviors.

I hope that you will try some of these methods if worrying presents a challenge for you. I care! Be assured of this. And besides, you wouldn't want me to be worrying about you, would you?

Lesson 4

BLAH! BLAH! BLAH!
TURN OFF THE CHATTER

"Never miss a good chance to shut up!"

That's what Will Rogers had to say. He was a humorist, actor and cowboy, popular in the 1920s and 30s. Maybe he was before your time. I like this quote so much. It fits right into these weekly lessons.

Think about this: If we are not actually talking or listening to some form of chatter, our minds are all too happy to fill in the space. Tearing from subject to subject. Interjecting thoughts, judgments, and instant analysis of any old thing. Playing the same tired tapes over and over. Don't we grow weary with all the activity? What a relief to shut up and take a break.

How would you feel about giving some time to silence? Does it seem strange to you? Does your mind object? Who IS the one doing all that thinking, after all? Who is there in the stillness? Could there be someone who witnesses all the falderal? Is it possible that you've been so busy with noise that you haven't noticed that some one else is there? Could it be YOU? Maybe it is time to get acquainted with the true you, the silent one who is in every moment of your life—waking, sleeping, thinking, and dreaming.

I am curious. Does it feel like you are meeting another part of yourself as you dip into silence? Or, if you have been meditating for a long time, maybe you can venture back into the time when you first noticed that someone—YOU—was watching. Most of us are astonished that there is someone other than the prattling mind within us.

In that stillness, when all the blabbering has stopped, you may notice that something subtle and powerful begins to happen.

"To the mind that is still the whole universe surrenders."

These are the words of Lao Tsu, the venerable Chinese philosopher who lived in the fifth century, BC. and is the author of the *Tao Te Ching.* His wisdom has resonated through the ages and carries much commonality with other spiritual and religious paths.

Of all the topics I have covered, one has drawn the most readers and attention. It is the easiest of all. It is based on the above quote. And then there is this:

"Be still and know that I am God."
—Psalm 46:10

Silencing the mind. Being still. Resting in the quiet. Isn't it an irony that *this,* the stillness, is the way to find peace and Truth? Especially as we live in a world ever more addicted to activity, noise, and interaction? We have filled our lives with chaos, with traffic and cell phones, with texting and talking, with 24/7 news feeds, with headsets and busyness. Do you think this has made us lighter and happier and more loving?

In Week One, we gave ourselves this reminder, to repeat over and over: I love myself completely NOW. For Week Two, we scanned our bodies to wipe away tension and stress. During Week Three, we targeted one of the thought habits that causes stress and discomfort: worrying. Now we take this week to choose the wonder of silence.

How simple! How novel! To do nothing. To just BE. To let go of activity and thoughts. To turn off the television, the radio, the phone, the conversation. To be by yourself as your Self. You know, you have never had to do anything or become anything to be the Light of your own Soul. You already ARE that Light. All by yourself. Just as you are right now.

There is profound power inside the heart of your own being. If you are already used to this, you know what I mean. If you meditate or commune with nature or pray, you know this. For many of us, the idea of just being with ourselves is strange, uncommon, maybe even uncomfortable or frightening. But it is worth the effort to go into silence, even if for only a minute or two. Throughout this course, we will explore many different ways to bring this to fruition.

Remember that whatever you do, you will let go of judging. You will be accepting and loving to yourself without exception. You will be light and kind to yourself. Everything will unfold in just the right way. Count on it!

For this week, here are some ideas to explore;

- Choose a time, anytime, today, to be quiet. Let your body soften. Feel your breath deepen and smooth out. Pay attention to a calming thought as you coordinate your breath with this thought. It could be one of these: "I love myself completely NOW." Or, "May I feel peace and be at ease." Or, pick a sound like *Om* or *Amen* or

Shalom or *Salaam*. Notice how they all have a common sound within them. This is no accident. The *Sanskrit* sound of *Om* or *aum,* is said to have enormous power within it. Just be quiet for a minute or two or three. Then go about your day.

- Choose to do the above a few times a day. Go somewhere quiet. Tell your family you are having quiet time. Perhaps they will want to try it out on their own. Just remember, this is your quiet time. All yours!
- If you already meditate (and good for you!), maybe you will take just a little more time this week. You can honor yourself for choosing to go within and love yourself even more.

So, for this week, all you have to do is enjoy a little peace and quiet. That's all.

Lesson 5

SOMETHING YOU ARE DOING RIGHT
NOW CAN CHANGE YOUR LIFE

There is something you are always doing that affects your level of happiness and peace and has a great impact on your health. Take a look at the number of times you do this one thing that is so significant to your well-being:

16 times a minute, 960 times per hour, 23,040 per day, 8,409,600 times per year.

Those are some of the numbers given for an average person. If you have not already surmised, we are talking about breathing. Yes, breathing! It is a given that we breathe all our lives, but the question becomes one of HOW we breathe.

As a yoga teacher, I learned this maxim: "If you can control your breath, you can control your life." That's a pretty hefty statement. In fact, there is an entire science devoted to breathing. It is called *pranayama,* and we who practice yoga learn to do a myriad of breathing exercises. What is important here is that, simply by learning some easy ways to alter your breathing, you CAN be less stressed and happier in your everyday life. So here we go!

THE BREATH

Feelings come and go like clouds in a windy sky.
Conscious breathing is my anchor.

Thich Nhat Hanh, a Zen Buddhist monk who has written countless books, made this statement. The breath is his anchor. Think about that. You can always return to the breath. It is with you all the time. You can learn to use it as a tool to alter the quality of your life. None of this is difficult. You simply have to be aware of it and use it. You will feel and notice change. I promise! For beginners, here are a few pointers:

- Pick a time when you can be quiet, even if only for a few minutes. Pay attention to your breathing.
- You want to be breathing in and out through your nose, not your mouth.
- Is the breath steady—in other words, is it even? Inhalation and exhalation? If the exhalation is a bit longer, that is okay.
- Do you pause and hold your breath between breaths? Try to keep it going, like a constantly moving wheel. Inhale, then exhale.
- Is the breath jumpy, jerky, and agitated? Think of each breath as smooth and silky. Flowing with ease.
- Keep breathing this way whenever you think of it.

Those are some breathing basics. You will find that doing this practice often will be calming to you. It will take you out of the world for a little while and put you into the present moment. That is always good.

If you are ready to add this next idea, see how it feels.
- While you are breathing like this, repeat our first affirmation—I love myself completely NOW. Coordinate

it with the breath, as if it were swimming on the wave
of the breath.
- Take Lesson Two and do a little body scan. I bet you
will see that your body relaxed right along with the
breathing .
- Add Lesson Three, if you are focusing on the breath,
you are unlikely to be worried about anything.
- And you are being quiet, so Lesson Four is in effect.

How easy is that? Remember, you don't have to spend much time
on this, but you do need to start to change patterns of breathing
for a more joyous life. In fact, every single day for more than
twenty-five years I have done special breath work just to stay in
check. Even seasoned yoga people could use this reminder from
time to time. We all can use this gentle reminder.

When you own your breath, nobody can steal your peace.

Peacefulness is much to be desired. Yet knowing how to work
with your breath is a skill that can save you in times of crisis.
Here is such a life-changing story:

One of my yoga students told me this years ago. She had taken
classes from me for a long time. She was aware of the power
of the breath and how to effectively use the breath in life situations. What she told me illustrates just how valuable it is to
know how to breathe properly.

She received a telephone call and was told that her husband
was in the hospital. He was in a serious condition, perhaps having suffered a stroke. She rushed to the hospital emergency
center. As she entered the building, where there were two sets
of doors, she walked through the first automatic door and was
about to go through the next door. She stopped herself. She
knew she was panicking. She remembered our lessons about
the fight/flight response and how you can control this through

17

your breathing. She knew that if she didn't do something right away, she would next be seeing her husband. He would know that she was frightened. Her mind would not be able to function in a methodical, calm way in order to make the right decisions for him.

Here's what she did: She consciously checked her breathing. It was high in her chest (fight/flight breathing). She made it deeper and moved it into her belly. Then she slowed and smoothed out the breath. In moments, she brought her breath *and herself* under control. By the time she entered through the second set of doors, she was calm enough to handle whatever she would encounter.

Now *that's* a skill worth knowing. See how powerful the breath can be!

How are *you* breathing right now?

Lesson 6

ON ETERNAL LOVE

Love is the essence of all true spiritual beliefs and paths. At least, that is how I see it. In touching the power and energy of that love, miracles occur and all else fades into the background. LOVE IS IT! Love is the reason for our very existence and the purpose of our time in the world.

In Lesson One, Week One, I asked you to repeat an affirmation about love as a means to open your mind, thoughts, and heart to a transcendent Truth—that you are loved beyond conditions and in a way that is not altered by time and space. I love myself completely NOW. That is the phrase and mantra. Did you say it? Did you feel the shift? Do you continue to say it?

Now we move to another lesson on love.

LOVE IS ETERNAL

If we believe that love is something that is time-limited, the pressure to know and experience it becomes restricted. You better figure it out between birth and death because that's all you've got. That's your life on earth. I used to think that. That is, until I was pushed—sometimes unwittingly and reluctant-ly—into a new reality. Now I know that we have all the time in this world and thereafter to get this. You have an eternity to get it. Love is actually the only thing, ever, you have to get. But, having said this, why not start right now? This minute! What is holding you back?

We are speaking of a love that goes beyond everything else. It is not some saccharine, schmaltzy kind of love (though that is not excluded), not some cheesy movie idea of love, not some self-serving love that expects something in return. This love is not a negotiation. It is completely of an open heart that gives without expectation of return. And this is the best part. You already possess this love within you, even if you are not aware of it. You might even be able to share this love AFTER you leave the body.

Some years ago, my dear mother took her last breath, and, under the light of a full moon, she parted the veil and moved into eternity. My husband and I were by her side, telling her how much we loved her at that moment. There is so much to say about the miracles that surrounded her passing, but I will only say now that she has sent us, (both my husband and me) hundreds of cheery and funny signs and messages since she departed this world. We don't think of ourselves as mediums or anything like that so this was more than a little surprising to us. After we got over feeling weird about all of these "coinci-dences", we pondered why these happy messages kept coming. We can only conclude that my mother is making sure we know that she loves us all the way from heaven (or wherever she is enjoying herself these days). I would call that a celebration of Eternal Love. What do you think? Has anyone who has passed sent you a sign or message that you saw as an indication of comfort and love to you?

Come on, you might say, we are born, we die, and that's it. Life and love, at least for the individual, is contained in that short space of time. Look, who am I to try to persuade you? There was a time when I would have agreed, even debated this side of the issue. But that was then, this is now. So many proofs have come along for me over the last years, and now I firmly embrace the truth of Eternal Life and Love. Mind you, a lot of study and reading has gone into this shift. Yet the clincher was a burst of wisdom that can only be called an awakening.

Just for a moment, think about what it would mean if you, YOU, were eternal. And not just eternal, but situated in the light of love. What does this say to those who have lost loved ones and to those who are near death? What kind of hope and joy might that provide on all fronts?

Here now is the assignment for this week:

- In a moment of quiet, maybe just before getting out of bed or before falling asleep or perhaps as you take silent time to meditate, imagine yourself as a being of light, surrounded by love. Let it be a circle of love that flows through you and all around you. Nothing but love moves within that circle unless YOU invite it in. Feel the safety and comfort in your "circle of love."
- You might like to enlarge your circle of love. Visualize it growing to include your home and everything and everyone in it—your family, your pets, your objects. Don't analyze who and what is in it and not in it. This in UNconditional love. Everyone is in it!
- Now enlarge even more, to include your neighborhood or street, then your city or town. Send out love freely, to everyone and thing in your country, then further to include the whole earth and beyond. No discrimination! You cannot leave out those of opposing philosophies or ideas.

- Here is another way to share this love. Imagine that it flows all through your past, touching and embracing everyone you have ever known. Then let it move into the future, to everyone and everything you will ever meet in your life.
- And after these experiences. Let it all go, without expectation. Send it into space, the universe, Divine Consciousness. Let the Love be so great that you don't need to be attached to it. Open your heart and let it go...

See this love as huge. Bigger than anything you have ever experienced. You have this power and energy. Do you think that "little old you" can't possibly do this? Think again! Try it.

It is written in *A Course in Miracles:*

*"God is but love
and therefore, so am I."*

Ponder that thought and see what happens.

Love is such a deep and rich topic; there are many avenues to take in discussing it.

We know that throughout our lives, love receives more attention than almost any other four letter word. It is bandied about. Some people celebrate Valentine's Day, with cards, flowers, chocolates, maybe negligees, and abundant expressions of love. Love spans the spectrum. Love of family, friends, country, pets, shoes, champagne, God—we love "love." If this is so, then why do so many of us have trouble loving ourselves? Have we given up? Did we really do so many bad and shameful things that we are forever excluded from honoring, respecting and loving ourselves?

*"We are all born for love.
It is the principle of existence, and its only purpose."*

These are the words of British Prime Minister, Benjamin Disraeli, written in the 1800s. How profoundly true those words have remained throughout time. Our ONLY purpose is love. And we must start with ourselves. Only by knowing and loving ourselves at the most deep and spiritual level, can we be at peace.

So far in *The 52* we have engaged several methods to let love for ourselves take hold. Think of it. We have tried:

- An affirmation—I love myself completely NOW.
- Visualization and imagery—Love flowing into you on every breath, filling you and spreading a circle, as large as you want, all around you
- Using the mind to give thought to the concept of love and how to understand it

Now we will expand our thinking even further. This time we will engage a process of releasing and reprogramming in order to more deeply love and offer compassion and kindness to ourselves. This is how to do it:

- Once again, choose a quiet and restful time when you will not be interrupted. You are going to think of a time when you, yourself, felt bereft of love. Maybe you were a child and had been reprimanded. Perhaps you, at any age of your life, felt angry or ashamed. You might have done something to hurt or harm another person. It could have been long ago or just yesterday.
- Now form a picture of yourself in your mind. Look at yourself, apart from all the judgments that you may have attributed to yourself in that situation. As if

witnessing this person, you, imagine that you can look at yourself with forgiveness and kindness.

- Engage your circle of love and let it flow with abundance into the "you" of the past. Imagine that you could hold and embrace, comfort and nurture the "you" you see.

- Say to the one you have brought into your mind. "I love you completely right now and always have." You know, Divine Consciousness /God has been saying those words all along, but you are now saying it yourself. Say the words. Mean the words. And then, when you are confident that you have healed your past image, let it be released with freedom and love. You may want to repeat this a few times, especially if you feel skepticism with any part of the process.

Notice how you feel after this practice. See if there is a sense of liberation and warmth. You can repeat it as often as you wish, with different scenarios each time. This is a powerful, healing method. You are, in fact, healing your present self by healing your past self. In future lessons, we will explore more methods that will use your physical body to aid in healing and loving yourself.

You see, the circle of love is not just for the present moment. It is beyond time and space, and you have the power to send it forth. You can love yourself ALL the time. You need not be dependent on someone else to give you this love, it is already yours!

Lesson 7

THE WORLD IS AS YOU "SEE" IT

How DO you see your world? Is it a place filled with love and light and joy? Or is it threatening, angry, frightening and full of pain? Maybe it is a sprinkling of both, depending on the situation. For most of us, it is not black and white.

There is a Siddha Yoga guru who has deeply influenced my life. I never met him while he was in his body, alive in the world, but he surely made his presence known in the most surprising and creative ways. It seemed as if he "lived" at my house, in my yoga room, for many years. His name is Swami Muktananda and he said this:

> *"People become what they are according to the*
> *attitude they hold in their mind,*
> *and that attitude is what they project into the world.*
> *Whatever worth you yourself have, you project that around you,*
> *and that is what you see."*

In one of his lighter writings he said that you have your own set of glasses and that is how you see the world, so be sure you have the right prescription. I think of this as a bit of yogi humor.

Do you realize that the way you see the world is different from the way everyone else on the planet sees it? Your world is colored and influenced by every experience you have ever had. And what you see can be altered and changed. You have the capacity to change how you relate to what you see. You can see the world anew and bring forth that which nurtures and comforts you, which calls forth the depth of your spiritual being.

We are speaking now about the sense of sight—what your eyes see—as well as your emotional reactions. Most of us take all of this for granted. As if we were passive, it happens to us. But STOP NOW! There is more to this than meets the eye. Soon I will write about *pratyahara*, an important limb of true yoga which deals with the control of the senses. But for now we have something to try.

"Seeing" Your World

Think of all that you see around you, the objects that take up space and flow around you. Much of this may seem out of your control—what you see as you drive your car, the people walking around you on the street, those who surround you at work or school or in your own home. In time, we will learn to practice the art of equanimity, staying in balance no matter what surrounds you. For now you can choose to surround yourself as much as possible with a circle of that which is positive and uplifting.

Here are some suggestions:

- Right now, take inventory as we learn about sensory input. What your eyes see, in this case. Think about it. What do you see around you when you wake up? In your kitchen? In your office? Are there visual items that are agitating to you? That make you uncomfortable?

Do you turn on the news and see images that upset you and make you angry or uncomfortable? Do you do the same on your computer? Become aware of what you voluntarily bring into your field of vision.

- Now think of what you can change or improve in your surroundings. What can you actually put there? Perhaps you will choose a photo of someone you love. Each time you see it, it brightens your mood. Maybe a soothing piece of artwork, of nature, of something with spiritual presence. How about an object that makes you smile that sits on your desk or kitchen counter. Be aware! Begin putting into your presence those things that can make you lighter and happier and more loving. That is, after all, the purpose of this course.
- Now begin to delete and replace. Let your sense of sight serve you in a spiritual way. You need not be some victim of circumstance in these matters. Turn off the TV if it unsettles you. Shake things up. See what happens.

I used this method to good effect in helping my elderly mother. Whenever she went to the hospital or was ill in bed, I made a special effort to put family photos near her bed, to add flowers and objects she could see whenever she opened her eyes. It was a little gift so if I wasn't there, all of these reminders of love were there all the time. I even found a stuffed toy, a Siamese cat, to lie with her on the bed in lieu of the much beloved living Siamese cat she had to leave at home. Did all of this help? I like to think so.

Use your own personal history. Be creative. What could you be seeing right now that will bolster your happiness and joy? It may seem like a small thing, but, believe me, it is not!

On an even deeper level, we learn that we see and create the world around us. Think of it like this:

Seven billion pairs of eyes look out on their world and believe they are seeing what is there. No two of them will see the same thing. Oh, sure, there may be agreement on the name of an object but what is attributed to that object will not be the same. This is because we are the ones giving meaning to all that surrounds us.

Pratyahara (the control or withdrawal of the senses) is one of the eight limbs of classic yoga as described in the authoritative work that describes yoga, *The Yoga Sutras.* This important book, written by Pantajali, holds in its pages much of the essence of yoga. It outlines the true path, far beyond the way most Westerners understand yoga, which is mostly yoga poses and the breath. In the course of our studies, we will give focus to these lesser known aspects of yoga, most particularly *dhyana,* meditation. But now for a glimpse of *pratyahara:*

If you meditate, you may have familiarity with the sophistication of withdrawing the senses. For those new to this idea, I like to first bring attention to the senses, so that we can begin to recognize their influence, use them for our benefit, and then proceed, if we wish, to withdraw from them completely.

The Truths that emanate from so many spiritual disciplines, like yoga, lead to experiencing the world in ways not generally recognized outside of the spiritual realm. For most of us, it takes some time to realize that the world is not what it seems to be. Our rational, left-brain thinking is not attuned to seeing in these new ways. Let's try this:

- Look around you. See all that is present. Leave nothing out. Think of the names of all that you see. You had to learn these, you know, as you grew up. They were taught to you in your own language.

- As you see them, ponder any emotional reaction you have to what is around you. This, too, you had to learn through experience and teaching.
- Now notice that everything you see is defined completely by you—in its name as you learned it and in your emotional reaction to it. In this sense, you created it as it is.
- Now see if you can imagine that all that you are seeing is neutral, without a reaction. Let everything be neutral for a while. Does this seem odd?
- Relax your eyes. Let them close. Is everything still out there even if you aren't seeing with your physical eyes?

That's all you have to do for now. Whatever you experience, just ponder it. All of this that you see seems to be outside of you. Or where is it really? Perhaps it is only in your mind. For now we are just playing with concepts. Stretching ourselves a bit. Testing reality. In time, we will consider seeing again, but on a different level.

I hope you are seeing these lessons as interesting, entertaining, and maybe even curious. All of that is good.

Lesson 8

ALL ARE WELCOME ON
THE PATH OF LOVE

"Come, come, whoever you are—worshipper, wanderer, fugitive
It doesn't matter—ours is not a caravan of despair
Ours is a caravan of endless joy!
Come—even if you have
broken your vow a thousand times
Come, come yet again. Come!"

These are the words of the great Islamic Sufi mystic and poet, Rumi. While his language was Persian, we are fortunate that the translations of Coleman Barks, who is also an inspired poet, are available to us. Barks captures so eloquently the beauty and the spirit of Rumi's words, which are among the most beautiful poems ever written and are filled with divine and ecstatic love. His translations of these poems will surface often in these lessons.

Years ago, when I visited Rumi's shrine in Konya, Turkey, I knew almost nothing about him and had never read any of his writings. Yet, when I walked into the shrine, the loving energy was so profound I burst into tears. At that time, I had no idea why I responded as I did. It took me years to understand the richness of his words, to experience that unconditional love, and to recognize that Rumi was to become for me a guide to teaching Divine Love. Now I ask you to join me on this journey!

You see, all are welcome on the spiritual road. It does not matter who you are or what you have done. No one is turned away, ever. None of us can pretend that we have not made mistakes, said or done something hurtful, or felt a sense of shame or guilt. Yet we are ever invited to come back to love.

Our first lesson was to repeat the affirmation, "I love myself completely NOW." Perhaps you felt that saying these words would be false, that you are not worthy, or that sometimes you are worthy but not at other times. But you ARE worthy, always, in the site of Divine Love, of Consciousness, of God.

There is a powerful story in the Bible that tells of a woman who is accused of adultery and is sentenced to the punishment of being stoned. Jesus intervenes and says,

> *"He who is without sin among you,*
> *Let him cast the first stone at her."*
> —John 8:7 King James Version

Whether sin is a concept you accept or not, we have all done something we wish we could undo. We are all in the same boat, so who are we to judge another? Instead we might engage compassion, kindness, and forgiveness—for others and for ourselves as well. Imagine how different we and the whole world would be under those conditions? And what if, just maybe,

sin was never a concept in the first place.

NON-JUDGMENT AND DIVINE LOVE

One of the first lessons I teach in my yoga classes it to let go of judgment—of ourselves and others. As most of these classes have included doing yoga postures (asanas), many students find themselves measuring against others in the class or against themselves. I should be more flexible, they might say, or look at how much better I am than she is, they might think. But judgment is never warranted and we learn in time to see everyone else as a reflection, as one soul meeting another. Indeed, at the conclusion of each of these lessons and my classes, my salutation is "Namaste," the traditional greeting that means, "I bow to you" and in the purest sense, it expresses a joining of our spirits in union and respect. It is a greeting from one heart to another, from one soul to another. Namaste!

For this week:

- Become aware of times when you are judging yourself harshly. Instead, remember that you are always in the Divine circle of love. Repeat the affirmation—I love myself completely NOW and mean it.
- If you harken back to actions and times when you denied yourself this love, reframe your thinking and see yourself bathed in love and acceptance.
- Be vigilant in noting judgment. Sometimes we are blind to a habit of judging and let the unbridled damage continue. We only hurt ourselves in this process. Take action. Change the way you see yourself.

Resolve to remember that you are never outside the circle of love, that, even when you stumble (as we all do) you come again, as Rumi suggests. You get back on track, "in the saddle," and keep going. We are all in the caravan of endless joy when we learn to shift our awareness. Come. Come yet again.

Dr. Wayne Dyer is one of the most prolific writers and teachers on the subjects of psychology, Divine Love, and the spiritual path. I have enormous respect for the way he blends spiritual truth, venerable writers, gurus, and poets' quotations, and his own unique humor and personal experiences into such a powerful message that seems to be applicable for all of us. He said:

> *"You do not define anyone with your judgment.*
> *You only define yourself as someone who needs to judge."*

I heard Dr. Dyer speak at an event in New York City. He held the audience spellbound for nearly three hours as he shared profound spiritual truths in the simplest language. He described how, as he became aware that he had just judged someone, he decided to correct the situation then and there. Many of us find judging so normal in our lives that we don't even notice. We just engage the behavior, gossip, devalue others, and pat ourselves on the back for our superiority. Or we notice and "fix" it. Or maybe we see the judging starting, but we are tuned in enough to delete the behavior right away. Then there is the step where the judging does not even start.

Where do you fit into this picture?

Let's make it a lesson:

- Do you find yourself routinely judging others, complaining, and arguing without any conscious awareness of this behavior? (Well, if it is unconscious, you might not be able to answer this part at all.) Let's say you are in a check out line. The person in front of you is slow at everything. They can't find their credit card or their cash. You are in a hurry and are seething inside. You might be calling them names to yourself or sighing and giving dirty looks. You think this is normal and you are justified. What's wrong with this incompetent fool, you might think.

- Next step: Do you see it happening and, rather than letting it go, you put a checkmark next to the behavior? Now you know you are doing it. You notice how angry you are getting and act just as in the previous description. But now you have noticed and something does not seem right to you. You are not behaving "normally."

- Let's say you notice it and it has affected another person. Can you correct it right now? You've noticed that the person in front of you in line is aware of your behavior. She has heard you sighing and seen your angry face. You stop and look at her. You stop the behavior. You say something like, "I think I am having a bad day," or, "I don't know why I am in such a rush," or you give her some indication that you have calmed down and you mean it! Maybe you even try to help her.

- Now you see the judgment starting and you are aware enough to nip it in the bud. You just plain stop it! You know that this is a situation that would aggravate you. Your blood starts to warm up but before it can start to boil you relax your body and your breathing and you back off.

- Let's say something happens that would normally trigger your judging, like the scenario we are exploring. You can let it go. You can smile within and remember the old judgmental you and then smile again at yourself. Now the check out line becomes a pleasant and learning experience because you have made it so. Congratulations!

Can you see yourself feeling softer, calmer, more loving? Do you start to notice that you have a lot to do with how you see and experience your world? Don't you feel better?

I used the example of the check out line because it used to be a trigger for me! My impatience and tight scheduling (along with a big dose of ego) would bring about those reactions. I would think ridiculous thoughts about how efficient and organized I am. What was wrong with everyone else? How about you? What is a trigger point for you? What might you find to use as a learning experience? I wonder. But I'm not judging! After all, who am I to judge?

Now there is another step we can take. If we are all connected, all beings in a bond of love, then what happens?

"We do not judge the people we love."

So wrote the French existential philosopher and playwright, Jean-Paul Sartre.

These words hold a great fascination for me—and maybe for you as well. If we see a world where everyone is connected in divine spirit to everyone else and that love is the binding element, then wouldn't we suspend the habit judging of each other? We would still hold the capacity to witness, to stand by in a state of equanimity and observe all that is around us, but we might engage other thoughts in the process. Perhaps we would think of compassion, forgiveness, kindness.

Now this is the best part: If we do not judge the people we love, what about not judging ourselves? If we don't love ourselves then how can we possibly love others? Nothing is MORE important than learning to love ourselves if we are to spread love from the place within our own hearts.

Remember, we are all on the caravan of love. All of us are welcome. No one is left out or judged or thought to be too small. Groucho Marx, the humorist, famously said:

"I would refuse to join any club that would have me as a member."

Many of us would have to admit to this feeling; such is our measure of unworthiness. So let's just say that, if you want to join the Club, your invitation is waiting and ready. There are no enrollment fees, no tests to take, no monthly minimum, no nothing. You may not know it, but your seat is already there, waiting. With open arms, you are greeted. All you need is a kind and loving heart and the willingness to know who you are in the truth within you. How about it? Can you love yourself enough to join?

Let's continue some lessons in non-judging:

- Whenever you encounter judging yourself, freeze the image you are holding. In your mind, separate from the person in that image. Imagine that you could just watch as a witness. Walk around the one you are judging and engage compassion, forgiveness, equanimity. Let those feelings replace whatever judgment originally resided there. Be kind.
- Take that person, you, and let the circle of love lighten and brighten the one you see. Let it wash away any negative feeling.
- Now see yourself transported into the place where Love is all there is. Into the Club, if you like. Here, you are constantly bathed in the love of all around you. How does that feel?

I can remember times when I said or did something so embarrassing or humiliating and, whenever I thought of that time, my body would literally shiver with anxiety. That feeling took residence in my body and mind all over again. Over and over. I kept replaying it. And for what? To instill the negative emotion deeper and deeper? What a mistake that was.

We will delve more deeply into this subject in the future when we begin actually monitoring our thoughts and erasing the habit of retaining those old images.

How does it feel to stop berating and judging yourself? How does it feel to shine in the light of Divine Love? How does it feel to know that you are, and always have been, loved at the core of your being?

Lesson 9

MEDITATE: INTERRUPT THOSE FIFTY THOUSAND DAILY THOUGHTS

This was the title of a blog post I wrote some time ago. It is worth repeating. Can you imagine that your mind is rambling away with that many thoughts a day? What are we thinking? How could we have so much chatter going on, just filling up our minds (emotions and feelings too, by the way)? Wouldn't it be nice to take a break from all that blabber, most of which is repetitive and non-productive? Well, you are in luck—you can take that break. It is all within your power. It is called meditation, and it could be the most important activity you will ever encounter in your life, other than loving yourself all the time.

At the beginning of these weekly lessons comprising *The 52*, I promised I would offer you practices that would be simple and include reflections on the body, mind, breath, senses, and the loving spirit within each of us. I hope you have realized that spending even a little time on any one of these lessons can have surprising results. If you experiment with being quiet and stop doing, you may have felt your life make some subtle shift. Keep at it!

Breath and Meditation

Here are some words to ponder, written by the renowned medical doctor and gifted spiritual writer and teacher, Deepak Chopra:

"Meditation is not at all a way of making your mind be quiet; rather it is a way of entering into the quiet that's already there, buried under the fifty thousand thoughts an average person has every day."

What a relief! The quiet is already there. It is just waiting for you to slow down enough to notice. And in that silent retreat, when you step out of the world for a bit of time, miraculous adventure awaits you. If you already meditate, you know this. Good for you!

Meditation is, by the way, not some difficult or mysterious thing. Millions of people meditate every day. It does not require miraculous skills or even deep spiritual wisdom, and yet it is life-changing.

Here is the plan:

- Choose a time, usually first thing in the morning, just before dinner, or at bedtime. Make it known to anyone around you that this is to be your time. No interruption. No TV. No phones or iPads.
- Choose a place to sit where you are not slumped over but with your back straight. If you are in a chair, place your feet flat on the floor. In yoga, we would say, with the head, neck, and trunk in alignment. Rest your hands on your thighs or fold them together in front of you. Have your thumb and first finger be in contact. This keeps the energy within.

- Close your eyes and pay attention to calming the muscles in your neck, shoulders, and lower back. Imagine a stream of warming light moving down your body. Softening...
- Now pay attention to your breath. Feel the rising and falling, evenly inhaling and exhaling through your nose. If the breath seems restless or agitated, try to imagine feeling it becoming smooth.
- Keep focusing on the breath or on any comforting sound, like "so ham" or "om" or "I am" or peace or any mantra you may have used. Now let the breath and the sound join together in a seamless path drawing you into silence.
- Continue this for at least five minutes, once or twice a day. Don't be discouraged if you miss or your mind wanders (it almost certainly will). Avoid feeling impatient or judging. Expand the time if you are comfortable doing so.
- Just BE. Nothing to do. Nothing to improve. Just BE.

Remember, there is no such as a bad meditation, but each one may feel a little different from the others. Just go with it. Try this and see what happens. There will be more encouragement to come.

Of course, in the meantime you are loving yourself completely NOW—as you meditate—and in every single thing you do.

> *"Meditation is not a means to an end*
> *It is both the means and the end."*
> —Krishnamurti

Krishnamurti was an Indian-born scholar and philosopher, a writer whose work embraced no particular religion, but one who had profound wisdom in the spiritual realm. He stressed that world change could not occur through some exterior entity—be it religious, social, or political. Change had to emerge from within. While he never allowed himself to be described as a *guru,* a spiritual teacher who engages with a following, he was nonetheless, the voice of Truth to many.

Meditation, then, is both a practice, as something we DO to reach an END (some would say spiritual enlightenment and waking up), and yet meditation is the end itself. Not to get too complicated—we just do it.

In the lexicon of spiritual activities, meditation ranks at the top. In classic yoga, meditation (*dhyana,* in Sanskrit), is the seventh of the eight limbs. If we thought of them as rungs, only *samadhi* (the super conscious state) would rank above it. As I tell my students, I can help to teach the other limbs of yoga, like breathing and posture, but this state, described in many ways as realization or oneness with the Supreme, is not teachable. It comes to us by Grace. So you might as well just relax and meditate and see what happens.

Here's an idea:

- After you meditate, try writing down your experience. How did it feel? How did you feel before and after? Was the mind especially active? Are you more calm? More anything?
- Over time, you will see patterns forming. These will help you. For example, you might find morning meditation more pleasant and useful than evening. You might adjust your time to sit in meditation. It's your own personal preference.
- Not meditating at all? Maybe you will write a few words or think of why you have made this choice.

Remember, no one is judging! No one! Not ever! (Wasn't that the point of the last lesson?)

Perhaps a few more thoughts on meditation would be helpful anyway.

> *The gift of learning to meditate is the greatest*
> *you can give yourself in this life.*
> —Sogyal Rinpoche

These are the words of a Tibetan Buddhist Dzogchen Lama. He describes meditation as going home and revealing our true heart. His most prominent writing is a book I value greatly, *The Tibetan Book of Living and Dying.* His words resonate with a Truth that transcends any particular path, which is one of the goals of my own work—to show the commonalities between the many spiritual paths.

One of the most renowned and respected Christian writers of this or any era is C. S. Lewis, a favorite of mine. In England, he was an Oxford don who converted from doubt to devout Christianity. He even engaged in fantasy works of fiction. You may know him as the author of *The Chronicles of Narnia.* He said:

> *"We live, in fact, in a world starved for solitude, silence and private:and therefore, starved for meditation and true friendship."*

And this from the *Holy Bible:*

> *"Sing unto him, sing psalms upon him,*
> *meditate upon his wondrous works."*
> —Psalms 105:2

Some may see the last quote more as a contemplation rather than meditation, but the idea of meditation is frequently mentioned in Christian writings.

To many of us, meditation is associated as an Eastern teaching. It is true that many of Western faith are less familiar with the concept of meditation, yet prayer, while different from meditation, bears many of the same fruits. In most cases, meditation is a solitary practice. Even while I meditated in the company of thousands of others, it was still MY meditation. Its great benefit is the promise of an authentic experience of God consciousness. One to one, if you will.

So this is the purpose—Divine Consciousness. Yes, as other benefits, we can experience less stress, being more centered, lower blood pressure and many other healthful results which are not a small thing. But meditation can bring about union with a higher power, with Divine Love, with God, with Eternal Life. Now that is something really big!

Here are a few more suggestions for meditation:

- Follow the earlier suggestions for meditation. Now, as you prepare to meditate, ask for guidance and Truth. Ask for Grace. ASK! Let your meditation be encircled with love and kindness. Then just meditate. Stop thinking. See how this feels.
- Come to a place of acceptance. Let the meditation just be what it is. If your mind went off on a grocery list or a bill to be paid or the next action of the day, be accepting. Okay, that is how it was today. Just let the thoughts float across your consciousness, as if they moved across a screen in front of your being. In one ear and out the other.

- Don't give yourself a grade. "Well that was a lousy meditation; I might as well give up." In truth, just about everyone thinks that at some point. Let it go. Just keep meditating in whatever way you can.
- If you just can't meditate, for whatever reason, be okay with that too. Even long time meditators may hit a patch where they have trouble. Be kind to yourself. Everything will unfold just right.

Everything about these lessons is about reaching out with love. So love yourself whatever you are doing.

Lesson 10

ON GRATITUDE AND HAPPINESS

"You have no cause for anything but gratitude and joy."
—The Buddha

What treasures are right there for you everyday? What great abundances do you take for granted? What small little sights and objects are present, yet you give them no mind? What is already in your life that makes you smile and carries happiness with it? Perhaps it is the smell of the soap when you shower. Or your favorite music on the radio. It might be your cat lying in a sun spot on the floor. You know that you are surrounded with so much that, if you just notice, can bring you a sense of joy and happiness. Our lives can be transformed by an awareness of gratitude, and happiness follows with certainty.

This is, I think, such a simple, yet profound, lesson. Remembering to count our blessings is something every one of us can do. It just takes a moment to pause and bring into our conscious awareness the bountiful gifts that surround us. What awakens your heart and stirs happiness and contentment within you? I am asking you to pay attention. That is all you have to do, and this will be the joyous and easy plan for the week—to bring more gratitude and happiness into your life. Just wait and see what happens.

BE GRATEFUL AND HAPPY

The English author and philosopher, G. K. Chesterton, wrote:

"I would maintain that thanks are the highest form of thought and that gratitude is happiness doubled by wonder."

How our spirits are lifted when we truly appreciate all that is around us! There are so many reasons and ways to be grateful and to express that gratitude in words, deeds, and thoughts. The smallest little thing can bring a smile to our faces and make happiness manifest within us.

I have a friend who began a movement. He founded and organized something called the Happiness Club. (www.happinessclub.com) When I first heard of it many years ago, I wasn't sure how one could actually have a club that focuses on happiness. But why not? The alternative is surely not something to be desired—the Unhappiness Club. Who would want to join that? Yet many of us seem to be charter members of the Glass is Half Empty Club.

Maybe we need some training in acknowledging happiness. My friend, Lionel Ketchum, who likes to wear a tie strewn with yellow smiley faces, began this movement. Happiness Clubs have sprung up all around—some for seniors, for singles, for teens, for anyone and everyone. From Lahore, Pakistan to Lyon, France to Durban, South Africa, and spanning North America. We could all use more happiness worldwide. Lionel, with his good humor, said:

"You don't need a red cape or have super powers to be happy.

It seems that most people think you have to be super human to be happy. I think that being happy is super and it makes you more human."

These days, we have academic studies in Positive Psychology at Harvard University and a special kind of yoga called Laughter Yoga. Any way to enhance our happiness is a good thing. And gratitude brings happiness with it. In time, you may even recognize that just "being" is enough to bring you bliss and joy, and you will be able to be content all the time. But, for now, give this a try:

- Every night, before going to sleep, think of five reasons to be grateful. Five sources of happiness. Take out a journal and write them down. You may be surprised at how many more than five have filled your day.
- Keep it simple. Maybe you have had a difficult day. We all seem to have them sometimes. You can still be grateful for something. A comfortable bed. A hot bowl of soup. Someone who smiled at you at the supermarket. A bird singing in a tree. Anything!
- Make this practice into a shared experience with a spouse or friend, your children or parents, someone you text during the day, anyone. Spread the gratitude like joyous seeds.

I think you will be surprised at how your life is lighter and happier with this easy little effort. If you have never tried it before, see what happens to you. I am smiling already!

Lesson 11

A PRACTICAL METHOD TO
LOVE YOURSELF MORE

"The measure of love is to love without measure."
—Saint Augustine

To love without measure. Think of it. No yardstick. No beginning or end of love. It is always there, and you need do nothing to be worthy of it.

This is a given in the spiritual world. You can count on love. You can take it to the bank.

If this is true, then why do we have so much difficulty in accepting and believing it? Why do we seem to be constantly on a search for love? Why do we feel incomplete, thinking we are without it, even when it is already there, within us? Love comes with us. It is part of the fact of being alive. But somehow we have been lead to believe that we have to earn it, that we are unworthy of it, that there is something wrong with us. That it is "out there."

In our very first lesson, I asked you to repeat this affirmation— "I love myself completely NOW." It was to be stated at all times and under all conditions. Even when we feel ashamed, angry, fearful, and in situations where we might think that love has abandoned us—especially at those times—we are to say it and let it sink in.

We MUST believe in love. It is paramount that we know that we are forever loved. It is crucial that we let go of all doubt in this matter. Love IS the essence of life and the spiritual world. Love equals God.

Now for a way to use your physical body to enhance that love.

To Love and Accept Yourself

Some years ago, I took a course from Henry Grayson, Ph.D. He is an extraordinary teacher, clinical psychologist, analyst, spiritual healer, meditator, and energy worker. He is an ordained minister and the author of several books, the latest being *Use Your Body to Heal Your Mind*. He taught an extended course, and from him I learned to fine tune the methods of muscle testing (kinesiology) as a means of measuring levels of trauma and ego-driven unrest in the body and mind, and for the discernment of truth. While we learned about tapping and "touch and breathe" (as used in EFT, emotional freedom technique) and many other modalities for healing, one that has resonated for my students and is easily accessible to anyone is what I call the heart massage. It is a means of massaging the chest at the heart center and where the thymus gland is located. It soothes and draws power in the heart center and stimulates the thymus, which in turn, increases immune response and healing energy.

There are those times when we feel angry, guilty, upset—a range of emotions that seem to be steering us away from loving ourselves. We would say that it is the voice of the ego, that which conveys negative messages thwarting our remembering the love that is ever-present. You can pretty much count on this: anything not supportive and loving is probably emanating from the ego. When this occurs, we engage the heart massage. Here is how to do it:

- Find a comfortable, preferably private space. I recommend that you sit down though you could surely do this standing as well.
- Open your hand so that the palm will be able to be in contact when you begin.
- Place your hand at the collar bones, palm open. Begin to move your hand in a clockwise direction, circling on your chest.
- As you do this, say these words: *I deeply love and accept myself even if...*
- To end this statement, you will add to it words that express the ego's message or whatever seems to be blocking the love that is within you. For example, let's say someone has said something insulting and hurtful to you and it has disturbed you and made you angry. You might say the phrase above and add, "...even if I feel like a fool for feeling bad about those words. Even if I hate that person for hurting me so deeply. Even if I wanted to retaliate and say something hurtful back. Even if I felt I could not control my anger. Even if I fear that people think bad things about me. Even if..." and you run through whatever you feel that is negative, on all levels.
- When you have exhausted all the feelings, you say *I deeply love and accept myself under all circumstances (or no matter what).* Now you stop. You should feel relief

and feel comforted. You should have released at least some of the negativity.

· Remember that each time you do this when you are disturbed you must speak the exact words and all of them. Each sentence must begin with "I deeply love and accept myself." You are planting this in your mind and heart.

I hope you will try this powerful method. It works. So many of my students and friends use it. I have used it as the basis for deep change in my energy healing work with individuals. And now, more than anything, I want you to value who you are and the love that is already there within you.

And more thoughts:

"Conquer the devils with a little thing called love."

That's the observation of the legendary Jamaican musician Bob Marley. That "little thing" called love turns out to be a very big thing indeed!

Are you prepared to really love yourself? Regardless of circumstances? No matter how much you have judged yourself and felt lacking? Even if you worry that you will never be worthy of love—from others, from your family and friends, from your own self? Maybe you think you are just too imperfect, scarred, disgusting, unacceptable, terrible—a curse to everyone and everything? You are a person you hate and know that everyone hates you too. There is no hope of anything ever being different. People with severe depression can experience this level of despair.

Is it too extreme to imagine thinking all that I have described? Too impossible to imagine anyone coming back from such self-denial and self-hatred? Yet it happens, and not so rarely. Most of us go along feeling pretty good and then something—the big something—happens and we plunge into the ego's damaging messages.

It might be a small something that we use to berate ourselves. I can't find my car keys. Or I forgot to pick up the dog food. Or I overslept. Whatever it is, it is not worth blocking out the love that is pulsing and glowing inside of us. Don't forget that these are only thoughts. At some point we learn that they don't have much meaning in the spiritual realm.

Often times the judgment comes from those around us, and for some reason, we take it to heart. We believe them, even if we know it is absurd to do so. Think of bullying. It is reprehensible enough for youngsters, but it can happen to us at any age. I like the expression that "whatever someone else thinks of you is none of your business." It isn't, but few of us believe it.

We need a line of defense against attacks by others and ourselves. I urge you to engage the heart massage whenever you harbor feelings of loss of love. And bolster it by repeating the affirmation, "I love myself completely NOW." See yourself surrounded by love and protected. Engage an image of those you know love you (living or out of this world) and by God or Jesus or angels or saints or a totem or any higher power you trust.

In my life, I have had periods when I felt bereft of love. I have lived long enough and worked with enough people in my spiritual teachings to know that we can all be subject to this feeling. It hurts when it happens. We feel lonely and vulnerable. We might feel that we will never escape those feelings. That we have plunged to the depths, with no way out. But we don't have to stay there. We don't!

Trust me—the heart massage and the accompanying messages work! Don't spend another minute feeling separated from love.

I deeply love and accept myself even if...

Finally, remember that in the world of yoga we are all one. When you ask for love to become manifest for you, you may be surprised at how the universe will click the "on" button and you will be sent love. Just in writing these words, I am sending love to you right now.

But we are not restricted to only using this clearing for present issues. Now we will see that, if needed, we can retroactively clear the past.

A Course in Miracles is one of the most important books I have ever read. To say I read it is hardly the case, I have spent years studying every one of its profound words and deep wisdom. It transformed my life and explained mysteries of faith and spiritual truth in ways that I could readily understand. The resonance of its words blended with all the teachings I had long studied in ancient Indian texts, yet it is a Christian (Christ-based) text. I recommend it to everyone who asks how they may move forward on the spiritual path and love themselves more. In fact, I now lead Study Groups for *A Course in Miracles*. My heart sings as I see transformation unfold in individuals right before my eyes.

These are some quotes from *A Course in Miracles:*

> *"God is but love and therefore, so am I.*
> *Love, which created me, is what I am.*
> *Love is the way I walk in gratitude."*

Love is the essence, yet the course speaks about the intrusion of the ego and how it can pull us away from love. So the heart massage serves to dissolve the activities of the ego by stating clearly that we love and accept ourselves no matter what the ego throws our way. Do you realize how powerful this is and how your life could be changed because of it?

I hope that you have tried the heart massage and experienced its cleansing and clearing effect. You can use it in the moment, when something happens during your day. You can also use it retroactively. Here's how:

- In the past, even long ago, something happened that shook your core of love. It may have indelibly altered the course of your life. If it still unsettles you, it is not too late to dissolve the ego intervention and move into love.
- When you have the situation firmly in your mind, begin using the heart massage. Delve into all the feelings, emotions and fears you felt then, repeating each time that you love and accept yourself no matter what happened. Try to exhaust every single negativity surrounding the situation.
- When you have finished, see if you feel better. You might even give yourself a measurement—on a scale of 1 to 10—on how much you felt unsettled, then re-evaluate afterwards. Your assessment of the number should have decreased. When I work with others on this practice, we actually muscle test to do this measurement.

If you decide to try to clear past issues in this way, I recommend that you restrict this kind of clearing to only one or two at a time. You may be surprised at how altered you will feel in this practice.

In this lesson we have actively used our body to participate in healing and bringing love to the foreground. I always feel better after this kind of work. I hope that you do too.

Lesson 12

LOOKING FORWARD TO LOOKING BACK?

See the butterfly soaring toward the light? Are you soaring? Are you experiencing a metamorphosis? Are you lighter and happier, more loving than you were when you began reading these lessons? Lighter and happier and experiencing Divine Love—that was my intention in writing this course in spiritual transformation.

Have you found that some lessons spoke to you more than others? Maybe you like to use your mind to plant affirmations. Or perhaps the body and breath is your primary vehicle for change so using action is best for you. Or you might see silence and meditation, letting your mind rest, as a form that appeals to you. If you are uplifted by the word love and feel joy in even saying or thinking that word, then lessons on love would appeal to you. I would hope they all have a resonance for you. They do for me! I say that anything and everything that can bring light, joy, happiness and love into my life—well, I'll take it!

At the very beginning, I promised that these weekly lessons would be simple, yet profound. From the responses I have received when these words were in blog form, those are two words that are most often repeated. Simple, yet profound.

This lesson is for reviewing and resting. If some of the lessons moved you more than others or seemed to bear fruit—that is, you felt lighter and happier because you tried something new or revisited something you tried in the past—then return to those now. Make them your focal point.

But if you read them, found them interesting or boring, worthwhile or worthless, it really does not matter. All is unfolding with perfection. The light is still there, beaming within you. You are still, as you always were, the loving spirit with the flame in your heart.

You know by now that Rumi is one of my favorite, enlightened poets. His writings are so full of truth and love that my heart soars with every word. He said:

> *"Come to the orchard in spring.*
> *There is light and wine and*
> *sweethearts in the pomegranate flowers.*
> *If you do not come, these do not matter.*
> *If you do come, these do not matter."*
> —Rumi translation
> by Coleman Barks

Well, what do you think of that? All that matters is that you love yourself and flow with the purity that is in your heart. That is my wish for you.

Lesson 13

Do You Hear
What I Hear?

"And silence, like a poultice, comes
To heal the blows of sound."

In the 1800s, Oliver Wendell Holmes penned those words in his
poem, *The Music Grinders.* Can you imagine what he would
think today? Everywhere we go, there is noise and sound. How
do we respond to all of this sensory input? That is the subject
of this lesson, a continuation of the exploration of *pratyahara,*
one of the essential eight rungs of True Yoga. It is all about the
senses.

We have already spoken about the sense of sight. Think back.
In Lesson Seven, we delved into how we see and how we are influenced, often unwittingly, by all that we take in through the
sense of sight. Now we will spend some time on another sense,
the sense of sound.

Most of us go about our days giving scant attention to what we
are hearing. Sure, if a siren blares down the street nearby, we
will likely take notice. Yet while we are generally unaware of

the constant cacophony of noises and sounds around us, they influence our wellbeing nonetheless. Before you can alter this situation and eventually, we hope, be un-influenced by whatever sounds are around you, you must recognize what is "out there."

THE SENSE OF SOUND

Something to consider for this week:

- Explore what you routinely hear around you every day. What sounds do you find abrasive and unsettling? Are these sounds within your ability to control? In other words, you cannot stop an airplane from flying overhead. If an ambulance screams down the highway, you can't jump out and stop it. Crows calling in the trees will not heed your request that they quiet down. Accept these sounds. Trying to alter them is a waste of time. Just let them BE. You may even grow to smile when you hear them.
- What about noises you voluntarily bring into your space? The radio? The television? Your iPod? How about choosing a noisy place to have dinner? You can begin to alter these sounds by taking action. Turn off the incessant noise of the TV. Stop listening to music that is jarring. Go to those places where natural sounds are around you.
- Now give thought only to the sounds that are soothing to you and bring you a sense of peace and calm. Perhaps it is a favorite musical piece. Maybe you like the sounds of nature—the leaves rustling in the trees, the songs of birds nearby, the gentle drops of rain as they strike the roof, the babbling of a brook or the soft waves on a beach. Whenever possible, I prefer natural sounds or specific pieces of classical music or, my

favorite, chanting the sound of my mantra. What do you like?

- Make it a practice this week to surround yourself with sounds that calm you and bring you joy. See what happens when you begin to alter what you are hearing. If natural sounds appeal to you, you can open the window or sit outside or, if they are interrupted too much by lawn mowers and leaf blowers, you can find a good CD to play inside or on your headset. If you close your eyes, you might imagine you are in a tropical rain forest. I like to listen to a CD of such tropical sounds. Then I am transported...

- Remember that whatever you hear has a subtle influence on how you feel and your emotional state. The more you are surrounded by sounds that are music to your ears, the more happy and light you will feel. This does not mean you must choose only sounds that are quiet and meditative. You may want something fun and upbeat. For years I played a tape (yes, a tape) of folk tunes I purchased on a trip to Australia. They made me laugh and brought a happy energy. I also spent years chanting my mantra out loud whenever I could and playing that mantra constantly in my car. *Om Namah Shivaya.*

As you begin to really hear and listen, you will learn a lot about yourself and your world. Then, in the final goal of *pratyahara,* you may actually withdraw completely from sound. Then wherever you go, you will be focused within.

It is said that yogis can mediate in the midst of total noise overkill in the heart of Calcutta, yet never respond to those noises at all. They remain at peace. Brain wave activity, scientifically studied, substantiates this fact. You can do this too. If not, for now take baby steps...

Lesson 14

Eternal Life AND Love

"Springtime has returned.
The Earth is like a child that knows poems."
—Rainer Maria Rilke

We think of springtime as bringing renewal. As I write this, it is springtime in New England where I live. The sun is warming the earth and in response, green shoots are popping out of the soil. Woodchucks are emerging from their hibernation and foraging for sustenance. New, colorful birds are arriving in the midst of their travels. There is a song in the air and an expression of lightness in the faces of people enjoying the fresh air.

We think of springtime as bringing renewal, and it does. One of the Christian holidays that marks this time of year is Easter, the celebration of true re-birth, hope, and love. It is a triumph of eternal love. All of these qualities are worthy of celebration, not just in the spring, but in all seasons of our lives.

Perhaps Easter is not a holiday you celebrate. Even so, I believe that Easter is an important day for all of humanity. Why would I say this? The story of Easter and resurrection is immensely valuable to contemplate when thinking of the meaning and duration of life and love. I am enthralled with the story of the passion and the unconditional love that is predominant in the Easter story. Of course, I was raised in a Christian family and Easter, with all its pageantry, was a special day in my childhood. I liked searching for Easter eggs, eating jelly beans, enjoying a springtime dinner with family, and dressing up in new clothes that reflected the sunny days and flowers blooming. Our family album is full of pictures of my mother, father, and brother, all decked out in new Easter finery, with my brother and me clutching Easter baskets full of treats.

For many years, I discounted the story of Easter. Those were the years when I took a sabbatical from organized religion. In fact, I pretty much discounted all the stories of miracles and faith, Christian or otherwise. That was then. Now, again, I call myself a Christian. But right along with this statement I could equally call myself a *Yogi* and a believer in the mystical branches of all religions.

I relish the chance to say, "Happy Easter." The significance of the story of Jesus and resurrection, of eternal life and love, and of what this says about death (or no death, to be exact) resonates with the truths of the most ancient spiritual writings.

I have written quite a lot about eternal love. I hope you will take a minute to go back to Lesson Six that focused on this subject. It will give you a better idea of how I came to so firmly believe in the continuation of life after we depart the body, and why I have not the vaguest doubt that love is eternally the most important subject of all time.

So now, at this time of renewal and rebirth, we remember the truth that our souls are free from death. We only depart from our bodies, yet we continue to be the Divine Spirit and embodiment of Love.

ETERNAL LIFE AND LOVE

This is the Practice for this week's lesson:

- Take a bit of time each day to contemplate the idea of eternal life and love.
- Carve out a few minutes to sit in silence. Calm your body and your breath. Long slow breathing.
- Now contemplate these words from *A Course in Miracles:*

> *"You dwell not here but in eternity.*
> *You travel but in dreams while safe at home."*

- Think on these words. What does it mean for you, for those who have already died, and for those you love who will surely leave their bodies?
- What if you are already dwelling in eternity, but have failed to recognize this?
- What if you are safe at home all the time?
- What if you are, right now, the perfect embodiment of love, but you have confused this truth with messages from the world of dreams.

I do not pretend that this is easy material to consider, especially if you are seeing it for the first time. It is, nonetheless, the basis of most spiritual paths dating from the earliest writings that still exist.

This is where we are heading. And, whether you embrace these beliefs or not, it does not alter the Truth.

You are Love.
You are Eternal.
Life is Eternal.
Love is Eternal.

These words are not just meant for Jesus or Buddha or saints or *gurus*. These words are about YOU!

Lesson 15

SIMPLY BREATHE

"Your breathing should flow naturally, like a river,
like a water snake crossing the water,
And not like a chain of rugged
mountains or the gallop of a horse.
To master breath is to be in control of our bodies and minds.
Each time we find ourselves dispersed and find it difficult to
gain control of ourselves by other means,
the method of watching the breath should always be used."
—Thich Nhat Hanh

How are you breathing? Right now? Do I seem to repeat myself? Have you seen this in another lesson? And, well yes, I do repeat myself. Some lessons bear repeating. We will keep doing it until we do it right. Paying attention to your breathing is one of these lessons.

We have already talked about this basic function of living—breathing—and how there are subtleties of breathing that often escape our attention. How we breathe has a lot to do with how we feel and how we live our lives. For example, if we breathe shallowly, up in the chest, we may be missing the depth of our being and our lives. Or, if we hold our breath and stop breathing completely, we may be holding back our feelings and emotions. The breath is a great teacher—if you take the time to notice.

We want to experience the pleasure of breathing. The richness and joy of breathing. The breathing is right there with you all the time. You can study your breath and learn a lot about yourself. Remember, you are learning and witnessing, not judging or using breath as a way to castigate yourself, "Oh, look at what a bad breather I am."

Don't go into judging. Not ever. Let it go.

How Are You Breathing These Days?

Here is a simple way to watch your breath:

- When you breathe, does it seem that the breath is jumpy, agitated, rough? Or it is soft and smooth? Be a connoisseur of your breath quality. If your breath is soothing, then your mind and body are being soothed as well.
- Do you hold your breath between the inward and outward breath? If so, try to keep it going, ever-moving like a wheel turning.
- Are you aware of breathing all the way into the belly or do you hold it high up near the throat? Drop it down and feel the lower torso expand.
- Give yourself a cue to keep checking your breath throughout the day. At a certain time (e.g. every half hour) or in a specific location (e.g. when I take a sip of water).

- When you have a few minutes, try counting your breath. Inhaling, slowly and smoothly, to one count and out to the same count. Try five and five, or more or less. Increase the number over time.
- Then try this count: Five on the inhalation and ten on the exhalation. Exhaling is the easier and requires less effort than inhaling.
- Do this "breathing to a count" for several rounds. You will begin to notice how much more the breath responds to you.

It is amazing to think that something as simple as breathing can help to guide us in our lives. But it does! See what happens when you and your breath work in tandem—all towards a lighter and happier, more loving you. Remember that all of these practices are meant as acts of love—for yourself and for the energy you hold and exude.

Lesson 16

As You Think,
So You Become

If you really want to become lighter, happier, and more abundant in Love, maybe you should think about dropping some of those negative thoughts that lurk around in your mind. I am talking about the ones you have probably been carrying around for a long time. The ones that get replayed day after day and nip away at your natural state of joy.

Do you believe that your thoughts form your reality? Do you think that by changing how you think (like flicking a switch), it can actually make a tangible difference in the quality of your life? On the surface, it sounds too easy to be true. And yet it is!

Thoughts have power and energy within them. They have more power than most of us can even imagine, so it's worth paying attention to what you are thinking.

Eckhart Tolle has said:

> *"What a liberation to realize that the*
> *"voice in the head" is not who I am.*
> *Who am I then?*
> *The one who sees that."*

In upcoming lessons, we will delve more deeply into the question of who we are and who is the True You. For now, let's think about the "voice in the head." We are thinking about it, so thinking has a worthwhile purpose. Yet most of the thoughts we have are random, repetitious and even potentially damaging. Most of us pay little mind to how and what we think, even as those thoughts construct the person that we seem to be. It is worth taking note of what you think—about yourself, others and the world around you.

THOUGHT MONITORING

Here is the beginning of a practice I learned from a man who has spent years as a therapist, author, energy healer, and teacher. He is Henry Grayson, Ph.D. and the author of several books. I introduced you to him earlier, in Lesson Eleven. I was a student in a course he taught several years ago, covering many methods of energy healing. We learned his program for thought monitoring. It is so worthwhile. This is it:

- Notice what you are thinking frequently during the day.
  If you are feeling agitated or any level of discomfort,
  check to see what you are thinking at that moment. It
  will likely be a negative thought and something that is
  unsettling to you. Put a "check" next to that thought.
  Note that it may be a recurring thought that keeps you
  locked into negative self-assessment.

- Now that you have pulled that thought out for investigation, label it. "Oh, there goes another one of those negative thoughts again," you might say. Now it is out in the open and no longer hiding from you. You have brought it out into full view.
- Ask yourself this question: "Do I want to continue to have this thought?" Do not analyze it. If the thought isn't good for you, you will answer "no".
- Because we know thoughts are repetitive and we've found this little culprit, this particular thought lurking in our minds, we want to find a way to get rid of it. So we say, "I choose to delete this thought." Or you can use the word "cancel" or "dismiss" or "burn out" or say words that seem right to you.
- Now that you have dropped the thought, you have created an empty space where that thought was —a vacuum. So now you will fill it with something positive, to form a habit of positive thinking. You could use the affirmation, "I love myself completely NOW" or something that puts a positive on the negative thought, or a mantra, or from *A Course in Miracles,* "God is but love and therefore so am I."

Experiment with this thought monitoring. Play with the words you use. Don't be shocked if you find that you have been creating a lot of negativity everyday by what you were thinking. Now you are "sweeping the deck" clean. Be patient and loving to yourself in the process.

This is a powerful practice. You may not tell everyone you are thought monitoring, though having a friend participate with you is a good idea. You can share the nuggets you find hidden in your mind, then watch as they begin to dissolve. You will be lighter and happier. Trust me on this!

Lesson 17

PRACTICE A LITTLE PATIENCE!

"Patience is the companion of wisdom."

Thus spoke Saint Augustine, the Roman Catholic saint and poet during the 1800s. Perennial wisdom does not change with time. Patience, it is said, is a virtue.

Most of my life I have not been a very patient person. I wanted things done yesterday. I suffered because of my lack of patience and my thinking that by doing more and more I could speed up time and make things happen faster. What I accomplished was a perpetual sense of frustration and a loss of living in the present moment. I was impatient for something to happen in the future. I am happier now as I learn to embrace the gift of patience. It is a very important step.

Take to heart St. Augustine's quote and these:

> *"With love and patience, nothing is impossible."*
> —Dr. Daisaku Ikeda,
> Buddhist Philosopher

> *"Patience and tenacity of purpose are worth more*
> *than twice their weight of cleverness."*
> —Thomas Henry Huxley, Botanist

PATIENCE

It may seem ironic that patience plays such a big role in success. Remember the story of the tortoise and the hare? Sometimes moving along at a comfortable pace is better than racing wildly. Action does not necessarily mean "right" action. And when you are patient in your endeavors, you save yourself all the anxiety that comes with impatience. You enjoy a modicum of steadiness and peace while pressing forward. You are okay just as you are, even while pursuing goals and dreams. You let go and surrender the fruits of your labor in honoring the "now." This is a whole lot easier than going crazy with fear. It is fear, in so many ways, that brings on impatience. If it is time you are worrying about, just forget it. We yogis say time doesn't exist anyway, but you don't need to take my word for it.

I promised that these lessons would guide you to a life that is lighter, happier and more loving. Sometimes we should focus on just resting with an idea, like a sense of gratitude for all that is so abundantly given to you—the sunshine, food, family, friends, the birds in the trees. Other lessons may ask you to take action, like monitoring your thoughts or checking how you are breathing or spending some time in silence or meditation. Yet there is a commonality in all of this: it is to be patient and love yourselves wherever you are at this moment. To love yourself right NOW!

- When you find yourself impatient to see change, to have an accomplishment, or to change yourself, stop for a moment. Rest where you are. Decide to see yourself as in the right place at the right time. You might say to yourself—No rush. Everything is unfolding in perfect timing. Breathe and relax, even when you look at that list of goals you may have right in front of your eyes.

- See yourself with loving and nurturing eyes, as if you could stand witness and view your body and your mind resting calmly and patiently.
- All in good time, you might say to yourself.
- What's my hurry? Especially if life is eternal.
- Smile at your impatience. Lighten up. You'll get there when the time is right.

We are not here in this life to be tortured with a sense of impatience, or to believe that once we have that thing we are impatient to achieve or experience that then, only then, we will be okay. You are okay right now. No waiting!

Lesson 18

JUST WHO DO YOU
THINK YOU ARE?

Just who do you think you are?

Here is the answer most people give to this question. "Well," they might say, "My name is Jane x. I live at x address. I am x years old. I was born in x town. I went to x school. I am a (fill in what you do—a doctor, a plumber, a housewife, a yoga instructor, etc.) My hobby is x. I am married to x and have x children. I am single," and so on.

You are describing who you are in the world. But is this who you really are?

THE TRUE SELF

In yoga and the spiritual world, those descriptions are interesting but not indicative of whom you are at the core of your being, on a transcendent level. Those answers are good to know if you are at a party and someone asks who you are. In the mix of meeting new people at some social function, you would probably not say to your inquiring new acquaintance, "Well, I am a transcendent and eternal being, completely perfect and bathed in the Light of Consciousness and God." Your new acquaintance would more than likely excuse himself rather quickly and move on to the next person and avoid you for the rest of the evening. You might want to stick to the conventional answers discussed earlier.

But what if the answer I just described (the spiritual one) actually *is* who you are? What if you are, in some way, *both* of these? As a human being, you are the commonly described one who performs functions in this world. But, on another level, what if you are much more than this? Could you imagine that you are the first one, the one we will call the "small self", and at the same time you are also the "Eternal Self"? And knowing this to be true, you can be in both dimensions.

Does this all sound a little crazy? It certainly did to me in the beginning. What does it mean if you thought of yourself as only the one you believed yourself to be all those years, (the small self) when you are actually something far greater and luminous than you could have ever imagined? There was a time when I would have seen this as total nonsense.

During one of my many readings in *The Yoga Sutras,* the classic book that defines the true essence of yoga, I actually GOT this reality, but it was not easy. I remember wailing and crying and trying to figure out just who this "Deanne" was, and what it meant if that was not who I was. What about my family? What about my cats? What about my history? I grieved for that "Deanne" and wondered what everything meant. Then, by some odd twist (or maybe it was Grace), I fell silent and into an exquisite state of unfathomable peace. Some might call it a peace which passed all human understanding.

Swami Muktananda wrote:

> *"You, the traveler, are what you are seeking.*
> *Everything is within you.*
> *The supreme inner stillness...is your destination.*
> *It is God,*
> *The Self,*
> *Consciousness."*

In his best selling book, *Proof of Heaven,* Dr. Eben Alexander, a neurosurgeon who was steeped in scientific theory, writes of his unexpectedly long and vivid near death experience. He encounters realms of existence and consciousness he could never have fathomed. After his recovery, he courageously examined what happened to him and came to the conclusion that the lessons he was given while out of his body, and which can be applied to each and everyone of us, were essentially these:

> *"You are loved and cherished.*
> *You have nothing to fear.*
> *There is nothing you can do wrong."*

I would call these lessons that describe true consciousness, the Supreme Self, which is who we are—far beyond our names, what we do, where we went to school and how much we have accomplished in the world.

Think on these ideas and take them to heart. Don't start judging them. Just for now, accept them at face value.
- I am loved and cherished just as I am right now.
- I have absolutely nothing to fear.
- I am already perfect at the core of my being. There is nothing I can do wrong.

Just try these ideas on for size. Imagine that the you who lives in this reality is always the you every day and minute.

Can you possibly love and accept yourself this much? Maybe you should get used to thinking this way. What would happen then? Maybe you, yourself, are perfect just as you are right now.

I think you are!

Lesson 19

AHIMSA: WHAT IF WE
WERE ALL NON-VIOLENT?

Ahimsa. What is that, you might ask? If you are a yogi, you would know. But no matter one's belief system, everyone benefits by understanding the depth of the word. *Ahimsa.* It means non-violence.

If there is something we could all use more of in this world today, it is non-violence. That, and true unconditional love.

The path of yoga is abundant with all kinds of valuable lessons on leading a loving and responsible life. We learn ways to work with the body, the breath, the senses, the mind, and how to "be" in the world. *Ahimsa* is one of those ways to be. It is a *Sanskrit* word that means non-violence. Most spiritual or religious writings have some kind of writing on this subject, whether they emanate from something like the Ten Commandments of Judao/Christian thought or Buddhist texts and others. We are asked to practice nonviolence.

In the *Yoga Sutras,* the quintessential book describing classic yoga, *ahimsa* is the first of the rules for living that are found in the *Yamas*. It is about learning to be non-violent in all ways. We are to remember that nonviolence is to be engaged on every level—in thought, word and deed, in all of our actions with others, with anything and everything in the world, and with ourselves as well. This broad definition reaches a profound level. To even scratch the surface of *ahimsa* can lead to significant change and may take years (or some might say, lifetimes) to fully reach its goal. It is a worthwhile effort.

Think about this. Not only should we not act in violence, or speak in violence, we should not even think in any way that could be deemed violent, abusive, hurtful, cruel, unkind, or damaging. Try this idea on for size. Think what would happen if we all engaged this behavior. Bullying would end. Tragedies of all sorts, Newtown and 9/11, no beheadings, no slaughter of innocent beings, no war would ever happen, and this is only scratching the surface. What about Syria, the Holocaust, the demeaning of women in many cultures? Child abuse, elder abuse, animal abuse would stop. And we would even end our own habit of self-denigration.

Think about it!

Thomas Alva Edison wrote this:

"Non-violence leads to the highest ethics,
which is the goal of all evolution.
Until we stop harming all other beings, we are still savages."

Non-Violence

If we are to be lighter, happier and more loving, as is the intention in these 52 lessons, then it makes sense that we take inventory about how we are treating ourselves, each other, and the world around us. If we are harboring thoughts of violence, even if only in our minds, then we cannot be functioning very well. Sure, we can put on a face that pretends kindness, while at the same time, festering within are feelings and expressions contrary to that friendly face. Or we might behave in ways that hide the self-violence of judging, demeaning and harming— maybe even *hating* ourselves. Violence is violence in whatever form it takes.

Many years ago, in my effort to do no harm and remembering the words of the great theologian and medical missionary, Albert Schweitzer, I was determined to do my best to avoid harming anything and everything. I noticed there were some moths in my kitchen pantry. Being clueless at the time, I thought they were clothes moths and wondered why they weren't eating my wool sweaters upstairs in the closet. I let them be. It wasn't long before I discovered the other kind of moth, the one that likes to invade the staples in the pantry. They were everywhere. In my flour, my grains, my cookies, my cereal. My determination for no harm gave way quickly. They were eating my food. They had to go, though I felt a measure of sadness in removing them. I guess non-violence and non-harming had reached its limit.

So we all have definitions about what is construed as violence. Let us explore this further:

- Trying your best to remain objective and non-judging (in other words, acting as an impartial witness if you can), think of feelings you may have that are violent and angry regarding yourself and those around you. Notice that these feelings are more than likely harming you just in the process of harboring them.
- Take one or two of these thoughts and see if you can diffuse them and let them go. Remember that everyone has challenges and that most people do the best they can to get by in the world. Who are we to judge them?

- Try to bookmark any recurrent thoughts of violence or hatred that flow through your consciousness and then with each of them, follow our earlier lesson in thought monitoring. Note the thought. Decide if it is constructive or damaging to you. Make the conscious effort to delete or banish it, then replace it with something loving.
- Do not use this lesson as a form of further self-denigration! This is about learning how you respond in life, and trying to make positive changes so that you are more open to loving yourself all the time.

Most of us change in increments, in baby steps. Removing one violent thought, behavior, or act has an impact larger than you might realize. Try it. I predict the very act of trying will lead to a lighter and happier, more loving you.

Lesson 20

LOVE IS LIKE A RIVER

Love is like a river. Continuously flowing and leading into the welcoming ocean of love. This metaphor is often used in song lyrics, in poetry and in spiritual writings to describe the never-ending, always flowing, and continuous love that is there to embrace each and every one of us.

Many rivers flow into the same ocean, just as many souls (seemingly separate) reach the ocean, only to see that they are all the same, glistening brightly together. They are the embodiment of love—from start to finish and then into eternity.

You flow on that river of life. You reach the ocean. You do not need to wait to reach the ocean to know this Truth. You can be conscious, awake and in full realization that you are now just as you always have been. You are LOVE.

THE POWER OF LOVE

There is a gospel group we have come to enjoy over the years. My husband and I have listened to so many of their songs,

89

we can now repeat the lyrics from memory. The music of the Gaither Vocal Band is exuberant, uplifting, and healing. When the music starts, in seconds our toes are tapping, our hands are clapping, and our spirit is soaring, even at times when we are confronting issues like grief, loss or sadness.

Their song, "Love is Like a River" is readily available on YouTube. It tells us that love runs and rolls from a lazy stream, keeps moving through the mountains and valley and over "everything in between," until it is finally, flooding and washing all over me. It is an ecstatic song of love and I recommend it highly.

The lyrics express the mighty force of love, ever flowing. If it hasn't already, it will be washing all over you sooner or later. Be ready to joyfully bathe in the experience. You will be carried on the current, buoyed by the ecstatic nature of endless and unconditional love. The best part of all this is when it finally hits you, that you have always—and in all ways—been both the recipient as well as the source of this love, your heart will sing!

Unfortunately, many of us spend more time listing the reasons we are not loveable, not worthy, not good enough. Instead, do this:

- Right now, make a little list in your mind or on paper of some of the loving qualities you have. They can be big or small. Maybe you showed kindness and love to someone lately, or opened the door for someone to pass through, or volunteered your time for a cause, or simply smiled at someone who looked like they needed it.
- Think of specific times in your life when you have felt love in your heart—for another person, an animal, a plant in your garden, a small child you passed on the street.
- Think of how you felt when love was extended to you.

- See yourself as a fountain of love that can flow from you, and then send it forth. In your mind, see that love entering into another human heart.

You see, you yourself are the river of love if you put your attention on it. BE that river and let it flow. Imagine how many hearts will be opening when they see that love coming. Don't hold back. It is an endless stream. Let it wash over everything in its path.

My heart is sending love to you right now. Are you getting it?

Lesson 21

SOME TOUCHING THOUGHTS

What does the word "touch" mean to you?

You might say, "Oh, I was so touched by your gift." Or, "I used to watch the TV show, *Touched by An Angel.*" You could go to a practitioner for a kind of body work called Healing Touch. Or you may make a conscious effort to get in touch with someone who is sick and ailing or saddened with grief. You might pet your cat or dog because that contact, that touch is soothing and beneficial to both human and animal.

The sense of touch is one of the five senses that include sight, sound, taste, touch and smell. In earlier lessons we explored the senses of sight and sound. Now we give particular attention to touch and what it means to us in the world and also in the spiritual sense. In yoga, we study one of the eight limbs of classic yoga called *pratyahara,* the control of the senses. We learn new ways to be conscious of how the senses impact our lives, how to use them to enhance our everyday life, and ultimately if we wish, we learn to detach from them as much as possible.

The Sense of Touch

The skin is the largest sensory organ of the body. It is our outer coating and provides us with valuable information. It protects us by sensing pain so we don't burn ourselves on a hot stove. It registers the comfort of warmth when the sun soothes our bodies on a cool day. It tells us that we need to put on a coat when we walk outside and feel a chill as a cold wind strikes our bodies. It acts as a source of pleasure when we are touched by certain people in certain ways.

Research has shown that people *need* to be touched in order to thrive and be happy. Years ago a study revealed that children in an orphanage did not thrive if they were not held and touched. Indeed, some even withered from the lack of touch. Perhaps even as we age, we are prone to a kind of emotional withering if we aren't touched in some way by those around us. Notice that we may shake hands on meeting someone new, or hug and give a kiss on the cheek or an air kiss. A high-five is a form of touch, as is a pat on the back or an athlete awarding another team member with a body bump.

But what does all of this have to do with a spiritual life and becoming lighter and happier? We can learn to use the sense of touch to improve and enhance our lives. Here are some ideas:

- Think about the clothes you wear and how the fabrics feel against your skin. Do you wear wool sweaters even if they make you itch? Do you choose stiff fabrics or structured clothing that is not comfortable to wear? Do you wear skin tight jeans, even if your body is stuffed into them, just because they make a fashion statement? Think about what you put on your body. It is your decision. Why not be as comfortable as possible?
- Do you take into account the temperature around you so that you do your best to feel comfortable wherever you are? Do you prepare and dress in such a way,

taking into account the weather, the temperatures and your activities?

- Aside from comfort, what feels *really* good next to your skin? A fluffy, soft, fleecy thing? A cashmere sweater? A cozy bath robe? A silky shirt? Soft cotton shorts and tops? Whenever you can, indulge this sense of touch.
- Do you regularly reach out and actually touch those people you love. Do they touch you? It is not too late to start if you feel you are lacking in this area.
- Could you make it a habit to extend your love to others by touching them in meaningful ways, holding a hand or touching an arm, hugging and embracing? I often think of people who may rarely be touched, such as the elderly or infirm or those with disabilities. It takes so little effort to reach out in kindness.
- Become a connoisseur of what pleases your sense of touch, not to be attached to it, but to bring pleasure.

I am keenly aware of the bonding created by touch and sound and sight in my interaction with one of my cats—Dilly, our handsome tuxedo cat. When I first wrote about him, he was quite elderly and ailing. Despite his frailty, I knew that he responded in a positive way when he saw me, heard my voice, and when I touched him. In his condition, this was the most important connection I could offer. We were both nourished by these acts of love.

It seems that we have reached a time when physical proximity with those we love and care about is often impossible. At one time, most families and friends remained in the same communities for their whole lives. Now family members and friends live in other cities, states and even in different countries. How do we touch each other? One of my friends uses the term "touching in" when she communicates by email. Under certain circumstances, it may be the best we can do to touch each other. While it is probably better to speak on the phone or Skype one another with visual contact, this is not always possible.

We can still touch each other through words and thoughts of kindness, support, concern, and love. It is better to do this than nothing at all. Here are some ideas:

- Send a card or letter to someone you love. It is almost a novelty now to use snail mail. One of my friends writes long letters on a regular basis. She is an artist, so she includes drawings and other expressions of her artful way of touching others. We are made happy whenever we see that something has arrived from Linda.
- Communicate by email or by other means. Forward a funny photo or a meaningful quote that will bring positive energy to others.
- For someone you want to touch when you are not present, ask someone to be your messenger, maybe a spouse or a caregiver. Some years ago, when my elderly mother was living with us, we went on a trip that would take us away for some time. A person who helped us as a caregiver for my mother stayed with her the entire time. Before we left, I purchased special cards, each with a handwritten note, to be given to Mom each day. My husband had a long-standing joke he and my mother shared. Each day he would secretly give her a piece of saltwater taffy, something she enjoyed. I say "secretly" because the idea was that I did not know about this; I had a kind of reputation for serving healthy foods. So, while we were gone, everyday our caregiver gave mother a piece of taffy from Richie, her secret taffy agent, along with a card from me. At least this was a special way of touching Mom with a special remembrance to cheer her. Oh, and a hug was to accompany all of this.

Be creative. And by the way, don't forget yourself. Book a massage for yourself if you can. Reach out and touch others whenever possible. Touching goes two ways. Or maybe even more ways—how about a group hug?

I will be very touched if you take this lesson to heart. See how much lighter and happier and more loving you will feel with observing yourself and the sense of touch. The more conscious you become about the senses, the more your world will change.

Lesson 22

THROUGH KINDNESS YOU ARE LIGHTER, HAPPIER AND MORE LOVING

Silent film star Charlie Chaplin was, in his era, a huge presence. Funny, controversial, outspoken and a film genius, he made waves wherever he went. And he said this:

> *"We think too much and feel too little.*
> *More than machinery, we need humanity.*
> *More than cleverness, we need kindness and gentleness."*

He had seen nothing in terms of machinery and technology as we do today. Imagine what he would say today.

LOVING KINDNESS

Now, perhaps more than at any time in the past, we must behave with kindness and gentleness. And this again brings us to using everything we have—all our senses, our minds, our bodies, our thoughts, and especially our loving hearts to acting with kindness under all circumstances, and most importantly with ourselves. Kindness grows from within. It reaches out to others and reflects on us. It soothes us to know that we can extend love, forgiveness, and kindness inwardly, not relying on others to do it for us. Kindness can become a habit, a natural way to respond in any event or situation. It surrounds us with a presence that merges us with the Divine Presence, with Divine Love, that knows *only* Love and Grace.

"Remember there's no such thing as a small act of kindness. Every act creates a ripple with no logical end."

This is a quote from Scott Adams, the creator of the Dilbert comic strip. I think it is very appropriate to consider. As many have written words about the simplicity of creating small acts of kindness, few speak of the ripples. Of course, even the tiniest act brings benefit to the receiver and the giver, yet it goes beyond. It moves into the consciousness of all of us, even as we may not have full awareness of this. In a profound way, each act changes the world and the hearts and minds of all of us.

If you think about it, extending loving kindness is so easy. Think about these questions:

- How hard is it to give a smile to someone you encounter during your day? It might be someone you pass on the street or even your own spouse or children.
- Is it really so hard to open a door for another person or to motion a car driver waiting to enter a lane to go before you?
- Is there someone you might call or email, just to say a few kind words?
- How about greeting those you see on a routine basis, like the checkout person at the store or the doorman in your apartment building or the neighbor walking the dog?
- If there is someone you know whose life has reached a place where they have few friends—perhaps because

they are old, without family, and most of their friends
have passed on, or someone who has made decisions
that led to addiction, or have without any act on their
own, been downsized in their job—maybe you could
reach out to them, with kindness and non-judgment.

- Or if all of this seems like too much, do you have a
spare moment to send some thoughts of loving kindness
to others? Thoughts! Just think love and send it forth.
Many of us believe that there is great power in such a
small act.
- Now do the same for yourself—in forgiveness, kindness,
love. Let the healing commence!

I am very enthusiastic about this kind of simple practice. In
fact, I so believe in it that I promise you that you will feel lighter and happier as soon as you begin. Give it a try.

I hope it becomes a habit. Watch yourself soar like the blue butterfly, right into the Light of Love!

Lesson 23

Do Nothing—All is Perfect

Nothing to do. Everything's perfect. Is that what I said?

Shouldn't you be changing yourself? Improving yourself? Fixing yourself? What about making yourself a better person, taking courses, working on yourself?

I will never forget when I first read those words in a Siddha Yoga course:

"There is nothing to do. Everything is perfect just as it is."

I was stunned. I don't have to DO anything? Me? Me, the one with so many flaws? Me? Surely, this advice must have been written for someone else—for someone much better than I am. It did not mean me, the one so far from any kind of ideal.

And perfect. Everything is perfect, just as I am right now? And, wait—forget about me, what about the world and the other people in it? Perfect? With murders, wars, terrorism, bullying, violence? And all of those frivolous, stupid, trivial, vacuous pursuits people follow? Perfect? What kind of craziness would lead one to give such advice?

Well, fasten your seatbelt; get ready to consider that this may be one of the best pieces of advice around. Laugh or shake your head if you want. Just try living with this advice, taking it in, and see what happens.

There is Nothing to Do. Everything Is Perfect Just as It Is.

As radical as this idea seemed at the beginning, I trusted the teaching I was following enough to use it as a start to daily meditation. I repeated it throughout the day. This was not easy for me, a classic Type-A personality, who believed that one should always be multitasking with at least three or four things going on at a time—like talking on the telephone while taking out laundry from the dryer while minding my dinner cooking on the stove and taking mental notes on the yoga lesson I had planned for that evening's session. Oh, and monitoring my breathing at the same time. If anyone did just one thing, they must be really lazy, I said in my judging mind.

The idea that I could do nothing at all, and I would still be okay, was unheard of in my assessment of life. That meant nothing to do or say or accomplish or prove or study or anything at all. Good heavens, would I even exist if I wasn't doing something? And to think that everything would be perfect with my not trying to fix myself (and everything and everybody else) seemed completely ridiculous.

Imagine! Just BEING was enough.

My ego, the haughty one who pretended to know a lot to cover up for the fear of knowing nothing and making a mistake, hated this idea. Being perfect (as in the eyes of the Divine) was anathema to the ego. Wouldn't I become like a bump on a log?

But I got to like the notion that I didn't have to do anything to be lovable, worthy—to just exist. In time I could relinquish and surrender enough to understand that I am not the doer anyway. That is just a game.

It did not turn me into a bump after all. I didn't go into a cave to sit and meditate all day. Ironically, I became even more capable and active, once I gave up being driven by fear and neediness. I was no longer swimming against the current, but flowed with the current. How calming and relaxing.

Then I came to understand perfection a little better. Studying *A Course in Miracles* and many other texts and writings showed me that this was not really my domain anyway. In the Course, it said:

> *"You are still as God created you.*
> *Nor can you dim the light of your perfection."*

Even if this seems whacky to you, what harm will it do to test it yourself? Here are some ideas:

- Repeat the following phrase as an affirmation when you rise in the morning and just before going to sleep: "There is nothing to do. Everything is perfect just as it is."
- During the day when you feel stressed, repeat it again. It does not mean that you will sit on a chair and do nothing; it means that you will take the tension out of your actions and accept some help—maybe from Divine Consciousness.

- In using the affirmation, remember that you are bypassing the ego, acknowledging non-doing and going with the flow of action.
- In trusting a certain perfection, you are also beginning to notice that what is in the world and what you perceive in your own mind are very much alike. Maybe this is a matter of *perception*. What if your perception shifted?

As I write this lesson, I know that these ideas may seem far-fetched to some of you. They may seem like spiritual gobbledygook. I thought that myself at one time. In fact, I had thought to hold this lesson back and write it much later in *The 52*. But now I think it is too important to hold off.

Every one of these lessons springs from a place of deep love and a desire to share information that, having been given to me (sometimes in quite miraculous ways) has made my life lighter and happier and more loving. Over time, I was unmasking so the true me could emerge. And that is my wish for you.

The Buddha said:

> *"If you knew how perfect things are...you would tilt*
> *your head back and laugh at the sky."*

How wonderful that is. Whatever is happening, we need to do nothing at all but rest in the perfection of consciousness. It sounds like bliss, doesn't it? And, of course, it is.

But what about those times when the world hands us tragedy, death, loss, illness, and our lives feel like we have been hit by lightning? What then? Can we still hold tight to our beliefs?

I used to think that those who are spiritually evolved, enlightened, would have reached a place where they are no longer subject to the challenges the rest of us must face. Somehow, Divine Consciousness, the Loving Light, God (call it what you wish) would shield us from all that would hurt us. While so ideal and something we would all long for, I came to recognize that this was a naive assessment. Anyone in the body, in the play of the world, faces tough times.

I can think of so many teachers, gurus, prophets, and saints who lead lives that were anything but easy. Recall that Jesus in some of His last words asked "Father, why hast thou forsaken me?" Even HE had moments!

Some people have suggested that pain and suffering offer a doorway to more spiritual understanding. I myself was unmistakably given this message in several mystical ways when the quote by Khalil Gibran kept appearing to me while I was in the midst of terrible suffering. This is the quote:

"Your pain is the breaking of the shell that encloses your understanding."

Over the course of three days it appeared over and over in books, letters, and if you can imagine, it even appeared at a Chinese restaurant inside a fortune cookie. Who would write such a thing in a fortune cookie, my husband and I asked ourselves? But there it was. I wish I could have gotten something like, "Your life will be easy and you will be filled with joy." But no, I was being clobbered by the pain message.

Believe me, I am not enthused about having pain and suffering in my life. But these events come anyway.

The day after I wrote one of my lessons for the week, such a sadness occurred in our household. Our much loved and dear, elderly cat, Dilly, had reached a point of suffering from many problems—a growing inoperable tumor, serious respiratory problems, thyroid disease. He stopped eating even as I tried to hand feed him. He became lethargic and his eyes expressed sadness. The time had come to ask our veterinarian to come and help us ease him from his pain and from the world in the most humane way possible. My husband and I were very sad to see our long time family member close his eyes and depart from our world. Yet we knew this would be the outcome. It always is, with every living being.

Can I still hold tight to my beliefs? That life is eternal and that no one dies. That there is nothing to do. That everything is perfect as it is.

I can. I must! I am committed to the spiritual Truth, as I understand it. Certainly, it is sometimes easier to hold to this truth than others. And, when it is a challenge to believe, holding to it brings great strength and transformation.

What about you? "There is nothing to do. Everything is perfect, just as it is." What do you think of this statement? Whatever your response, it will be perfect!

Lesson 24

WHAT WILL YOU
HEAR IN SILENCE?

"You can hear the footsteps of God when silence reigns."

Sri Sathya Sai Baba spoke these words to share with us the depth of power and the healing grace of engaging in silence. Imagine the notion of being so close to the Presence, Divine Consciousness, to God. We don't have to be literal in interpreting Sai Baba's words. Even without belief, miracles can still occur.

We meditate to shut off the cacophony of the world and to go within. We turn off our iPods and computers, our televisions and radios so that we can be on our own, without the trappings of the world. For anyone familiar with the practice of silence, it is well known that the real adventure, the heroic exploring, is within us. But if we are addicted to the world and its busyness, we never experience or understand what is so special about resting in stillness. If you try it, you might meet with some surprises—like touching the essence of your own Self, your own transcendent wisdom, the True You. Anything can happen...

Silence is Your True Friend

My favorite Sufi poet/mystic, Rumi, wrote this:

> *"Now I will be quiet and let silence*
> *separate what is true and what is illusion,*
> *as thrashing does."*

Thrashing may not be a familiar term to some of you. It means to beat or hit repeatedly. It is also a farming term. Farmers thrash the seed from the husk, separating it from the hay. This I see as Rumi's intent in using the word—to find the kernel of wisdom while we are quiet.

You don't have to go anywhere special to engage in silence. Often we think it is necessary to go to a retreat, a meditation cave, a weekend seminar—somewhere other than our everyday life. You don't have to wait for a special occasion or event. You can start right where you are.

A weekly class I teach is called Meditation in Movement. We settle ourselves into meditation and then, while meditating, we begin to slowly start moving through yoga postures. It is paramount to recognize that the depth of meditation does not leave us and does not have to fit into a box or set period of time.

Here are some ideas that might prove useful:

- Choose an activity, usually something quite routine like riding a train or bus, drying dishes, or eating lunch, then stop for a moment and remind yourself to be quiet. Be in the present.
- You might become super conscious of your routine activity and let it become an impetus to be present and silent. At one time, during a period of upheaval, I made

driving my car the practice. I focused on every aspect of my driving—my hands on the steering wheel, my foot on the accelerator, watching for traffic. In truth, I was witnessing myself doing these things, but from a place of silence and acceptance.

- If it suits you, pick a specific time to be still. Early in the morning, before the world kicks in too much, just before dinner or at bedtime.
- Repeat the word "silence" whenever you feel the need.

We are learning, little by little, to "be." To hone our skills at altering our perception of who we are and what the world represents.

"Silence is the true friend that never betrays."

That's what Confucius said about silence. Who doesn't need a true friend that never betrays? A friend you carry around with you. You don't need to text them or call and make a date or go out for coffee with them. This friend requires nothing but your understanding that it is there at your beck and call and will never leave you. I'll take that kind of friend.

This friend of silence, peace and stillness offers even more. There you find a retreat from the frenzy and demands of the world. Like giving yourself a little vacation, you can be there in a place where you are appreciated and enjoyed, where there is no guilt or criticism. Wouldn't you like to spend a bit of time every day with this friend?

Elisabeth Kubler-Ross was a person deeply connected to eternal wisdom and love. She said this:

"There is no need to go to India or anywhere else to find peace. You will find that deep peace of silence right in your room, your garden, and even your bath tub."

What are you waiting for? An invitation to a retreat? You have it! A few extra minutes in the day? Maybe that will never come. A crisis that sends you into such despair that you must do something to find peace? Better to make it a practice for all times, good or bad, as you may experience your world.

Give yourself the gift of silence and peace. No one else can give this gift to you. You deserve it! And it is a worthwhile endeavor—one that can bring riches beyond your wildest dreams.

Lesson 25

TRUTHFULNESS MAKES FOR A LIGHTER AND HAPPIER SELF

Shakespeare wrote these words:

> *"To thine own self, be true and it must follow, as the night the day, thou canst not then be false to any man."*

Satya, a *Sanskrit* word, means truthfulness. It follows *ahimsa,* which means nonviolence. We focused on it in Lesson Nineteen. *Satya* is the second practice we learn in the *Yamas,* which are restraints or ethical guidelines on the path of yoga. So, if you thought yoga was merely a bunch of unusual poses with the body with some ways of breathing thrown in, you have missed the essence of yoga.

Yoga is and has always been a spiritual path teaching us to love ourselves, to release the illusion of duality and to reach a state of union with Divine Love and Consciousness. Yoga is rich in its age-old wisdom. The classic text, codified by a writer named Patanjali in the *Yoga Sutras,* offers a clear and brilliant road map for learning to live in the world, but transcending it at the same time.

In this course of 52 weeks, I promised to show how yoga and other spiritual paths lead us to the awareness of the True Self, the eternal core of our being that is ever blissful. This week, we introduce the concept of Truthfulness (*Satya*) and how you will be lighter and happier and more loving as your authentic self emerges more fully.

THE YAMAS: TRUTHFULNESS (SATYA)

Can we be consistently truthful in all activities of our lives? Is it possible that we are congruent in these three aspects—thought, word, and deed? In other words, do we have the courage and fortitude to be honest under all circumstances? For most of us this is a very tall order. You see, it goes beyond avoiding little white lies, it means being ourselves on all occasions.

When I first began practicing this limb of yoga, I actually thought it was about not lying. I did not recognize the depth of meaning. Then I heard people talk about the notion that, as Shakespeare said of being true to oneself, it meant being consistent under all circumstances. People spoke of the dilemma of acting in one way with certain people and in another way with others. Which one was going to show up, depending on the company? And further, if one projected a certain persona then switched to another, how was it possible to remember which character was being played and with whom? Putting on an act can be quite exhausting and confusing. Better to be authentic in all environments. It makes life a lot easier.

The same goes for telling lies. It seems that some people are very adept at fabricating stories, not just on occasion, but almost all the time. How they can keep track of their many stories confounds me, yet some are very good at it. The concept of Truthfulness for them is unfathomable; it seems they are addicted to lying and often actually believe their stories.

Let's consider some ways to analyze where we fit on the truth-fulness scale. Caution! I am asking you to avoid turning this into a way to experience guilt or self-criticism. We are wit-nessing who we are in a non-judgmental and forgiving way. This is merely a beginning point for making your life easier and more fulfilling. It is a way to feel comfortable in your own skin.

- When you are alone, are you a different person than the one who engages with others? Can you accept and love yourself in every setting?
- Do you find it necessary to play one role in certain company and another when with other people? If you do this, how does it feel when you are different from the one you are when you are alone?
- Do you feel the need to stretch or alter the truth in your conversation? If so, why? How do you feel?
- Do you think about who you should be, playing a role to be nice but not necessarily real? Do you make a habit of distorting or silencing yourself to please others? (This was one of my challenges. Many women, myself included, were taught to be people pleasers. I learned this early in my life.)
- Are you able to speak truth in uncomfortable situations while still remembering to engage non-violence and compassion? Do you think before you speak so that what you say does no harm to another? (Pausing, taking a breath, and witnessing yourself are all helpful.)
- On the subject of lying—do you find that you have difficulty being truthful about who you are and how you behave? Can you honestly evaluate yourself without placing harsh judgments at the same time?

Give yourself time to ponder these thoughts. It may not be easy, but I promise you that it is worthwhile.

When I began writing and sharing my beliefs and my personal life as a yogi, I knew that I was making a breakthrough into Truthfulness. Still, I sometimes felt vulnerable and worried about the response to so clearly stating these ideas. I knew that some of my friends had little awareness of what I really believe. So this has been an adventure into exposing my authentic self, and it has been liberating.

I hope that you too will feel this liberation. It is, I think, a courageous act and very worthwhile. And best of all, you will learn to love yourself even more in the process.

You see, in embracing the Truth of yoga and Divine Consciousness, we are already approved. We are pre-approved from the time we were born and even before. Not remembering this causes us to trust the ego more than trusting our inner core. Rather than embracing the light, we instead let fear inch its way into our awareness and behavior. As I learned early in my yoga training and study—fear is the basis for all of our suffering and misery.

Johann Wolfgang von Goethe, the renowned German poet and artist whose work, *Faust,* had a lot to say about Truth, said:

> *"The first and last thing required of*
> *genius is, love of the truth."*

You don't have to qualify on some random scale as a genius. Just knowing and living with this principle is enough. It makes you a genius in my book. But I am not saying it is easy. To be untruthful to others is one thing, to tell lies to ourselves is another. We can only try while still loving ourselves in the process.

So let go of fear. Move boldly forward with Truth in your heart.

Lesson 26

Devoted to Divine Love

What does it mean to be devoted to Divine Love and to actually feel that it defines who and what you are? There is an entire area of study in yoga that follows this path. For me, it is the most joyous and simple.

Shyamdas, a great devotee and follower of Divine Love, was honored in a memorial gathering as I was first preparing to write this lesson. Earlier in the year, Shyamdas was involved in an accident while in India where he lived most of the time. I learned of his death when I saw a Facebook post from someone who was with him at the hospital when he took leave of his body. As soon as I validated that it was true, I called his mother, my friend, Gloria. I felt privileged to be invited to the memorial tribute held in his honor.

The day of the gathering was a beautiful sun-filled afternoon, the time of the summer solstice and with a full moon rising. Somehow, everything felt auspicious, almost as if the space was energized by a special brightness. We gathered in a tent in the garden. The sound of *kirtan* (chanting) softly welcomed the many of us who were invited. There were family and friends of various faiths, many of whom knew Stephen Schaffer as a young Jewish boy who frolicked on the lawn where we were now seated. Others knew him as Shyamdas, a *bhakti yogi*, who wrote and translated scores of books, was a musician, artist, and *kirtan* chanter of renown. His unbridled love of Yoga and God made him an exceptional teacher.

He spent much of his adult life in India. He didn't follow the pattern of many yogis of his era (and others named "das") who returned to live in the United States and developed a large following. Although some of this happened later in his life, in most cases seekers went to him— people like Sting and Trudy Styler, Madonna, David Life and Sharon Gannon (the founders of *Jivamukti Yoga* in New York), The Beastie Boys, and others. He was welcoming to all.

There is much to learn and appreciate when considering the life of a *bhakti,* one who ecstatically sings the praises of God, lives in that praise, and sees that all of us are part of Divine Consciousness. The times I met and spoke with Stephen (as I knew him because of my relationship with his parents) were not the simple ordinary settings. One was the memorial gathering for his father, and the other was a wedding reception for him and his new bride. In those days, I don't think I quite understood who he was and what he knew. Even as we spoke of yoga then, I was still years away from knowing myself as the *bhakti* I would become. So what I experienced and learned during the tributes to him resonated with me for many reasons.

Divine Love

How would it feel to be embraced in a feeling of love and devotion most of the time? To witness yourself through eyes of pure love? To see the world as *lila*, God's play? To recognize the Divine in everything around you? To know that this Love is eternal and will accompany your soul even when you depart your body? These are some of the Truths that seemed so relevant during the memorial tribute.

Love is truly the message! It is the reason we all gathered together, to share a love for Stephen/Shyamdas and/or for the family and friends who grieved for him. Maybe that love was so great that the soul of Shyamdas could not contain himself. It felt that way as I watched various miracles unfold that seemed to spring directly from him. After all, that is what *bhaktis* do; the love is so big it explodes in the heart, especially if you are a chanter, singer, musician, as Shyamdas was. It becomes a living expression of that exuberant love. I am familiar with this feeling—of tears of joy spontaneously falling, of feeling connected to everything and everyone with a purity of heart, and of feeling home (as in h*OM*e) at last.

How can we apply this in our everyday life to be lighter and happier? Here are some ideas:

- When you rise in the morning and before going to sleep at night, spend a few moments considering the wonder of life. It could be in the form of gratitude or in something special that happened that day. It might be simple like how comfortable you feel lying in bed. Anything!
- Ponder the idea that you, yourself, carry the light of Divine Love within you all the time. Think of it as a birthright, as a given.
- Imagine that everyone you meet and everything you see is part of the Light and shares this Eternal Love. You might bring to mind someone you love and see them surrounded by this Love. Or, maybe even better, see someone who has troubled you or angered you, and see them equally that way.

- Put yourself into the most perfect, dreamlike spot you can imagine. Maybe at the sea or in the mountains or wherever you feel at home. See that place as a vista of God's Love, of *lila*.
- Try to hold on to this open-hearted Love, with complete abandon and joy. And, if sometimes you lose that sense of joy (which can happen to all of us), be kind and forgiving and know that the feeling will return. Just witness yourself without judging.

I don't know that these would be words of advice from Shyamdas, they are interpretations of my own feelings of *bhakti*. I think he would like them.

Here is something he wrote in his last will and testament:

"Jai Shri Krishna...What a lila!"
To my entire family as well as to my circle of satsang friends
and teachers:
It was an honor to be part of it.
Know that the soul is eternal and plays onwards,
always reaching for the Beloved.

Thank you, Shyamdas. We know your soul is very much alive, chanting even now. And as you say, *Om shalom!*

All of us can celebrate the feeling of Divine Love together. I feel gratitude in my heart for the experience.

Lesson 27

ARE YOU THE DIVINE SELF?

Marianne Williamson, the writer and popular spiritual teacher who was inspired by one of the most life-changing books ever written, *A Course in Miracles,* has shared these words:

"Our deepest fear is not that we are inadequate. Our deepest
fear is that we are powerful
beyond measure. It is our light, not
our darkness, that most frightens us...
We were born to make manifest
the glory of God that is within us.
It's not just in some of us; it is in everyone."

Why, oh why, then is it so difficult for most of us to believe and acknowledge this?

In the yoga world, we talk a lot about the Self and the ego. I used to think that I needed to work hard to recognize the Self (the divine presence) in myself. That I might be the Light of Love and Truth and Divine in any way seemed a huge stretch. Me? ME? Flawed me? Unworthy me? ME? Who was I kidding?

I would say to myself it would be lifetimes before I could even approach something so wonderful and self-loving as that. A few times I thought, why even bother?

Guess who was telling me all this? If you said, "the ego," you would be right. Of course, the ego is totally invested in bringing on guilt, shame, helplessness, and fear. That shadow side was ever ready, cloaking itself in oozing sweet words, so I wouldn't recognize it. Hiding behind trees and jumping out in various costumes, to masquerade as a logical, reasoned voice. When the ego wasn't showing off in cunning words, it was shrieking words so full of fear, I just knew I was low-down and a hopeless loss. At the time, I didn't recognize that I didn't have to listen to that talk, entertain those notions, or spend even an iota of time analyzing whether or not they had merit.

The ego, that nasty voice of doubt and fear, relentlessly tries to convince us that we are less than The Divine Light of Love. If we really, truly knew beyond doubt just how wonderful and complete we are and how much we are loved, the ego would lose its job. Imagine! Banished forever!

ARE YOU THE DIVINE SELF OR THE EGO?

Many years ago I thought it would be useful for my students (and for me) to draw up a list of what I considered some of the attributes of the True Self. This was the list:

Divine
Eternal
Blissful
Loving
Non-Judging

Content
Light
Calm
At Peace
Trusting
Perfect

I told everyone that these words express who we are at our core, and that for a quick glimpse of the ego, just apply the opposite of these words. I felt as if too much attention was focused on destroying the ego attributes, that it was better to focus on the good in all of us. One of my students memorized the words and repeated them as she took her daily walk, letting them sink into her consciousness. She said it helped a lot. Another student dropped a copy of the list onto the backseat of her car as she left class. Sometime later, her husband was in the car with her and spotted the sheet. Reading it, he asked if these traits were something she aspired to. She replied (and I love this), "No. It is who I already AM." Would that we all knew that all the time.

Here is an exercise for the week:
- Take any one or all of the words and see how they manifest within you.
- When doubt arises, remember that it is only the ego throwing water on your parade, diminishing you.
- The Divine Self is naturally perfect. That is how you are seen by the Divine. Don't get mixed up in thinking the word "perfect" is "egocentric."
- Apply these characteristics to others in your life. If you see them in this light, maybe it will be easier for them to experience this for themselves.
- Be patient with yourself. If your thoughts start running contrary to these attributes, try a little thought monitoring as described in an earlier lesson.

- Whatever your success level with this exercise, always end it with repeating, I love myself completely NOW!
- Oh, by the way, it takes some practice to get this. Be patient and kind to yourself. You might have already spent most of your life thinking just the opposite. It is never too late to change.

Lesson 28

WHAT DO YOUR
SENSES TELL YOU?

Have you any idea how profound the sense of smell and taste can be? Consider this. When there are bad odors in the air, people drive very aggressively and car accidents increase in number. Did you realize that, for most of us, when we are exposed to the scent of lavender, we experience a feeling of peace and calm? Examples are numerous!

Did you know that the sense of smell is 10,000 times more sensitive than any of the other senses, and that the response is immediate? It goes straight to the place where emotion and memory are held.

So watch what you are breathing—and tasting.

In yoga, we learn to examine the world around us so that we better understand how we are internally influenced. This is done in many ways, but ultimately we come to recognize that the play of the world does not define us. We come to know who we are as beings of Light and Love, but this is usually a process and does not happen overnight, even if we have recognized glimpses of Truth in an instantaneous fashion. Most of us need some help along the way, often in the form of lessons and steps.

The Eight Fold Path of Yoga is a complete system to bring us to awareness. In this lesson, we complete one part of it. It is called *pratyahara*. It is about learning to control the senses so that we can better focus on our True Self. We need to first understand the subtle influence the senses have on us, how to work with them and use them to enhance our lightness, happiness, and joy in living. We have already spent some time with the senses of sight, sound, and touch (in Lessons 7, 14, and 21, if you care to review.) Now we give attention to the remaining and more subtle two senses—smell and taste. They are surprisingly powerful and may influence you much more than you might expect.

THE SENSES OF SMELL AND TASTE

Whenever I smell cookies baking, I am back in my mother's kitchen at Christmastime, seeing her open the oven, removing the cookies and placing them out to cool a little so that I can taste one while it is still warm. I feel an overwhelming sense of love. Anytime I smell a fresh tomato, I remember picking them from my father's large vegetable garden, of his explaining about ripe tomatoes, taking them into the house and eating them right away. The remembrance fills me with happiness. The scent of lavender reminds me to be calm and restful. The smell of peppermint, even in the peppermint soap I sometimes use, energizes and lifts my spirit. Whenever I have a taste of chili con carne, it is football season in my mind. The roses I just picked from my garden always bring a feeling of love, romance, and beauty. Some say that when you smell roses, Mary, the mother of Jesus, is near.

What about you? What scents and tastes brings memories rushing into your awareness?

If the sense of smell were not so important, we would not have access to thousands of perfumes and colognes, to deodorant and breath mints, and even Odor Eaters. We are a smelling population.

I have grouped together the sense of smell and taste because they are closely aligned. Have you ever noticed that your enjoyment of food may decline if you have a cold and stuffy nose? Smell and taste work together. Smell is known to be the most powerful and primitive of the senses. It attaches to memory and emotion in a way that the others may not. It bypasses thought process and brings memory alive. It is the only sense that moves directly into the brain through the limbic system (the hippocampus and amygdala) and bypasses routine thought evaluation. Imagine the power! If one loses the sense of smell, usually appetite declines and food taste is different.

Because these two senses are so tied to memory, emotion, and survival, here are a few ways to become more keenly aware of their influence:

- Make a list (in your mind if you like) of those fragrances and foods you find pleasing.
- When you respond in a negative manner to either sense or taste, take note. Is a memory being tripped? Can you find a way to avoid the experience? Can you learn something of value from it?
- If you know your mood and sense of enjoyment in life is enhanced by certain smells and tastes, consciously make them a habit.
- If your routine requires that you be around smells and tastes that are unpleasant, how might you adjust your reaction to remain in a state of equilibrium and at ease?

• Can you see that none of these senses actually alter
who you are at the core of your being? Yet they can
enhance your life.

I remember hearing a story many years ago about a group of
followers of a certain esteemed guru who took them on a "conscious" walk. Their mission was to see everything as part of
Divine Consciousness, of God. As they strolled along the street,
a bus passed them, emitting a black cloud of noxious exhaust.
Everyone reacted, finding it repulsive, harmful to the environment, irresponsible of the driver—except the guru. She reminded them calmly that everything is part of the Divine—even
that.

So let all of your senses bask in Divine Light, even as you bring
more knowledge of the senses into your everyday life.

Lesson 29

STOLEN ANYTHING LATELY?

What? I am not a thief, you say. I don't steal. But it may not be all that easy...

When was the last time you were late to a meeting? Did you steal the valuable time of others? Has it ever occurred to you that hoarding—keeping more than you actually need, be it food, money, possessions, could be a form of stealing? Have you ever taken someone else's idea and pretended it was yours, taking credit that belongs to another? And how about stealing emotions from others—by pretending to be connected but actually being detached from them? Or having casual sex which was only casual for you and not the other person.

In this lesson, we continue examining the moral and ethical limbs of the Eight Fold Path of Yoga. This is one of the *yamas*. We have already spent time with the first two—non-violence and truthfulness. Now we turn to *asteya,* non-stealing. As you have seen, there is considerable depth to each of these concepts. That is how it works in this spiritual study of yoga. You can't just say in a flippant way something like this: "Me? I don't steal from people. I am not a thief." And maybe you are not and never have been. Let's see...

ASTEYA—NON-STEALING

From the first time I heard of the *yamas,* my mind went straight to the Ten Commandments. They were rules. You could take an inventory and check off the ones where you deserved a gold star and the ones that seemed a little iffy. At one point in my yoga practices, I went through each of them every single day just before meditating. I did this self-examination through the *yamas.* At the beginning, just as with the Ten Commandments, I think I did some kind of surface evaluation. It took a long time for me to recognize just how much depth there is to each.

Before saying more, please remember that these lessons are not meant to set up a sense of guilt or failure. We have already ascertained who you are at the depth of your being. That you are loved beyond measure and that it is the core of your being. But we still seem to live in the world. If we can better align our daily behavior with our spiritual Truth, we will certainly find ourselves lighter and happier and more self-loving. There will be congruity.

Swami Sivananda wrote:

"Desire or want is the root cause of stealing."

This is interesting to contemplate. If we are content with what comes to us to fill our needs, we will not be tempted to steal. Yet from the time we are infants we are surrounded with the notion that we need more, should accumulate more. Advertising and commercials ceaselessly tell us about all the things and experiences we don't have. On top of all that, the implication is often made that unless we have those things, what ever they may be, we are inadequate, unworthy. We don't rock. It is no wonder then, that we are sometimes willing to do anything to get them.

Here are a few thoughts to consider, remembering that you are witnessing your behaviors, not judging them:

- The most basic idea in non-stealing is whether or not you have knowingly stolen something that does not belong to you. This is not hard to evaluate, unless you steal without even knowing or thinking about it. If you robbed a bank or stole a purse, you know you have been stealing. If you put an article of clothing in a bag and did not pay for it, you stole something. If the cashier forgot to charge you for something and you knew it, did you steal? Just think about what you may have taken that was not yours, whatever it was.
- What about stealing of personal information, like passing on a confidence that was shared in trust by a friend.
- If you regularly play loud music or party late into the night, are you stealing quiet time from others?
- Do you repeatedly interrupt conversations to make your own point? Is this stealing?
- Do you steal from the environment if you use more of something than you need?
- How about stealing from animals or Mother Nature?

These questions are posed to broaden the concept of non-stealing. Again, they are not meant to evoke guilt or shame. The PC (politically correct) police do a good job at that already. YOU decide what makes you comfortable and how you feel. I might say that I could likely answer yes to many of the above questions—though I never robbed a bank or stole a purse. At least not in this lifetime.

Now, to move deeper into this subject, I suggest you consider whether or not you unwittingly steal from yourself. Does this seem impossible? We recognize that most of us function on two levels or planes while we are in the body. Even when we know there is something called the Self, that which is eternally free and based in love and perfection, we are all at risk for wavering. We may find ourselves in the clutches of the small self, the ego. Ego trips us up into believing that we are something other than what we really are. It causes us to believe that we are separate from one another. Because of this, we are capable of "stealing" from ourselves.

Do you find that you steal from yourself in any of these ways:

- Do you steal from yourself the opportunity to be quiet and calm when you engage in activities or mix with others who could disturb your peace?
- Do you find yourself eating foods and drinking beverages that could steal from an otherwise healthy, mindful body?
- Do you mindlessly steal from your spiritual life by letting the senses rule in ways that the culture may support, but your spiritual life may not? For example, do you spend hours watching newscasts or TV, sitting in movie theaters seeing violent or demeaning (to anyone) films, or listening to angry and jarring music or speaking negatively of others, etc.?
- Do you say certain words that you know are not your true thoughts, just to be accepted, and thus steal away your own truth?

Do not be mistaken by these questions. We are free to make our choices and let go of judgment. But you know, on some level, when too much is too much. Where is your higher self in all of this?

I hope that this lesson has been beneficial to you. I would never want to mindlessly steal away your time.

Lesson 30

REST IN EQUANIMITY, EVEN WHEN EVERYTHING ELSE IS CHAOS

This is one of my most popular and personally favorite lessons written before I started *The 52*. It seemed right to include it as one of the lessons. I hope you like it. But rest assured, I will be in equanimity, whether you like it or not.

Equanimity is the quality of being calm and even-tempered, of having composure. It means we are neither elated nor depressed, especially in difficult times. Other words that come to mind are unattached and undisturbed. Ancient Vedanta writings teach us that equanimity is our true, eternal nature apart from time and space, where we rest in the peace and love within our hearts. While equanimity is well-defined in Indian teachings, yoga, and Buddhism, it is spoken of in other spiritual belief systems as well. St. Paul writes in Philippians 4:11-13:

> *"I have learned to be content with whatever I have. I know what it is to have little and I know what it is to have plenty."*

Sri Sathya Sai Baba said:

"Let the wave of memory, the storm of desire, the fire of emotion
pass through without affecting your equanimity."

What would it be like if the ups and downs, the constant shifting
of good and bad, did not disturb your innermost being? What if you
could see all of these changes as nothing more than fluctuations
on a screen, as a kind of movie playing out before your eyes? For
most of us, this is a tall order. Life and death, good and bad, war
and peace, love and hate—all present challenges. They threaten
our inner perch of peace. Many of us come crashing down, falling
from that safe perch, and we are gripped in the drama of these life
events. Some are able to hold forth with steady wisdom most of the
time, then something dramatic occurs and our resolve crumbles. If
we know to honor and respect ourselves, setting aside harsh judgment and remembering the ways of being human, we can safely fly
back to our perch and remain gentle and kind to ourselves. We fell
off the perch for a while. So what?

In the *Bhagavad Gita*, the Lord says to the seeker, Arjuna:

"One who leaves behind all desires emerging from the mind
and is content in the Self by the Self is
said to be one of steady wisdom."

Swami Gurumayi adds the warning to "Watch your own mind.
Never allow it to get carried away by either pleasure or pain.
On the path of yoga, the path of steady wisdom, the path of
right action, steady wisdom is crucial. Become a sage of steady
wisdom." In our steady wisdom we discover a safe retreat. We
can rest there with trust. But be sure to note that equanimity
does not mean losing compassion in life or letting go of helping
others, but instead, all that we do comes from a place of peace
and calm within.

To imagine that we can control the constant changes that occur around us is a hopeless desire. We can only control our reaction to the play of the world, resolving to be the quiet space in the midst of stormy seas. Sometimes the buffeting of the winds is too much and we react. The pain of grieving, the unfairness of events, the fear for our future, or the depths of depression become too much to bear. Yet most of us recover our equanimity even if it takes time to do so.

My yoga students have an expression. They say, "I fell out of the boat." The story goes that we are all rowing the boat across the sea of *samsara,* across the sea of the world of change. At the helm of the boat is our spiritual guide, it may be a *guru* or Christ, Allah or God or, (how about this?), you as the True Self. Every once in a while we find the turbulence has become too much and we fall headlong into the sea. There we flail about, fear drowning, sharks circle us. We doubt that we will survive. Then, as if by some miracle, a hand reaches down. Our savior (or maybe even our Higher Self) pulls us up without any effort at all, smiles upon us, and puts us back to our rowing position, safe and on a steady course.

Seneca, the Roman philosopher, wrote:

"Happy the man who can endure the highest and the lowest fortune. He, who has endured such vicissitudes with equanimity, has deprived misfortune of its power."

So pause before taking an action or speaking a word. Are you responding and acting from a place of equanimity? This is a worthwhile practice and the benefits grow greater day by day. And on those occasions when you act or speak in haste, forgive yourself—then look to return to your pleasant and calm perch of peace. It will be there for you without fail.

For most of us, it is so easy to have our peace invaded. We give up our own sense of calm at the drop of a hat. Or maybe when we see someone drop a cigarette butt or candy wrapper on the sidewalk. "Litterer!" We might judge and feel indignant about it. We might feel superior to another whose habits do not match our own. Now I am not saying it is okay to litter, I am just asking if it is worth loosing your equanimity over it. Or because the person driving the car in front of you is slow? Or when something in the news is exasperating? Or someone arrives ten minutes late?

Just how important is it for you to stay with that which really matters. There you are, soaring like the blue butterfly, freely floating in the warm embrace of Divine Light, and then something trivial happens and you give it all up. You know you can make a choice. You can learn new responses. You can establish a peace that is not interrupted or bendable.

Think about this:

- If you can, count to ten before you react. Maybe it isn't a new idea, but this is time tested wisdom.
- Ask yourself, is this worth losing my sense of peace by reacting to it?
- You can react as usual, but as a witness. In other words, you might say, "Hey, please don't throw your candy wrapper there." at the same time as you let go of the outcome. You see yourself in a kind of play.
- You might spend time learning to meditate or recognizing that while you meditate you have a familiarity with your innermost being. Then, when agitation rises, you can easily send yourself right back to your peaceful place. You know that place so well; it feels like home to you.

Most of us are easily thrown off base. It does not have to be this way. Trust in your own Divine Wisdom of Kindness and Love. Always move outward from that very place and your life will be transformed.

Lesson 31

ARE YOU YOU
WHEREVER YOU GO?

Okay. I know I am paraphrasing Jon Kabat-Zinn, who famously said "Wherever you go, there you are." In fact he wrote an important book with this same title. His words are wise, and I recommend you take a look at his work.

Don't we often think that WE would be different if something around us would be different? Oh, if only I lived in Paris (or New York or India or Montana—fill in the blank). Or, if only I had a more understanding spouse, partner, mother, child (fill in again). Or, if only I had the time to study meditation or get my M.B.A. or take a vacation. You get the picture! If only . . . The grass is always greener, isn't it?

Or what about this? I am my most authentic, honest self only under certain circumstances. It emerges when I am with like-minded people. But are you the same one with your co-workers, your "superiors," your in-laws, your children, your parents, with ALL your friends?

ARE YOU YOUR AUTHENTIC SELF?

Many years ago I was teaching a yoga class at a health club. There were noisy classes in the next room and people gazed through the glass to see what this weird thing, yoga, was. One of my students, who I now realize was actually "really" realized and was an enlightened being, arrived at class early. I casually said to her, knowing that she had spent a lot of time in an ashram in India with a very famous *guru,* "Oh, it must have been so much easier to have peace and quiet and practice yoga in the ashram." I remember that she responded with a kind but heartfelt laugh and told me that it is the same everywhere. I did not have a clue what she was talking about. How could that be?

But it is true!

Some time ago, I returned from a weekend program at The Omega Institute in the rolling hills of Rhinebeck, New York. In the United States, it is considered a venerable place for learning, a kind of spiritual summer camp. The place overflows with synchronicity, with energies of past and present teachers of Divine Love, with crossovers on all spiritual paths. Hundreds of us were there to bask in the place and learn something new.

It was intriguing to hear one person after another say how happy they were to be with others who were open to whatever they were seeking. Over and over I heard the comment, "When I am at home, I almost never talk to others about this"—or whatever their focus was on the path of growing. "They just wouldn't understand." Such is the pity. So they were different at home. But at Omega, it was a safe environment. They could simply be.

Yet just like the most sacred locations in any part of the world, there emerged the ego identities we hoped we had left behind.

There were those who complained, those who brought their emotional baggage with them, those who found fault as they struggled to be something new or different, but it was not so easy. The beds weren't soft enough. The people in the next tent were rude and stayed up too late. The typical complaints as seen through their eyes only. I don't say this in judgment about the complainers, just observation. I know to the depth of my being, that everyone is the Divine Light of Truth and Love, steeped in compassion, gratitude, and forgiveness. That is the core that we can rely on, no matter where we are.

I don't pretend that remembering this truth all the time is easy. It takes a measure of trust and courage to be congruent at all times. I try my best but do not always succeed. I do see improvement however.

This helps me. I hope it will help you:
- Is it possible for you to witness yourself, as if you could stand aside and watch your own behavior in an impartial, yet kind and loving way? This can lead to a better awareness of who you are being at different times.
- When you know in advance that you may be in situations that will challenge your sense of Self, can you take a few moments to settle into your core— taking a few breaths or meditating for a while or saying an affirmation like "I love myself completely NOW?"
- Do you sometimes hear yourself say or do something that you know for sure is inauthentic? Can you simply mentally put a check next to it to revisit the moment later, to see how and why you took that action?
- Are you able to stay light regarding your behavior? In other words, not replaying over and over again those times when you felt out of sync. Lighten up!
- Finally, and only if this is not too astonishing to consider, can you believe that all (make that

everything) unfolds with Divine Consciousness and
that you are not the doer? Is it possible for you to
venture the thought that the world is actually a play or
maya?

These lessons are meant to help us find ways to feel lighter,
happier, and more loving in the world. When you operate from
your own truth, you will feel better. Your life will be more
smooth and easy.

Imagine being able to say and be who you are wherever you go!
It may take a little time to get there, but it is worth it!

Now, let's delve a little more deeply. How would you feel if you
absolutely and honestly loved the you who is present at all
times? Even when you know that you are not in the best form.
At those times when you realize that anxiety or fear has caused
you to be other than the you at the core of your being? Did you
know that you are loved unconditionally, regardless of how you
are performing at the moment?

It should be easy to know this and believe it. But, for most of
us, it isn't.

While we may strive to stay authentic and true to ourselves, we
all falter at times. I remember certain times in my life when
even the most trivial action could throw me for a loop. Things
like calling someone by the wrong name. Or missing an ap-
pointment. Or getting angry at some little thing, like a slow
driver in front of my car. Or not finishing everything on my
overloaded To Do list. (Didn't I actually fill it so full that I could
never, ever get everything done in one day and then would feel
guilt about it?) In the scheme of life and the world, these are
small glitches. They are tiny dots on the tapestry of life. What
was not operating for me was the loving witness—me. I didn't

realize that with just a little shift I could engage the love that is always flowing from my heart.

So be aware and know who you are as you are functioning in the play of the world. But never forget that you are the Light of Love, and no one can ever, in any way, deprive you of this Truth.

I am your fellow traveler on this journey. Love connects all of us. I am happy that you are with me.

Lesson 32

CAN YOUR BREATHING
HEAL YOUR BODY?

Thich Nhat Hanh, the Vietnamese Zen Buddhist monk observed:

*"Breathing in, I calm body and mind. Breathing out,
I smile. Dwelling in the present moment.
I know this is the only moment."*

Do you think it is important to calm the body and mind? Do you think doing this and paying attention to your breath can actually, tangibly change your mental and physical health?

For most of us, breathing is just second nature. We are born and we breathe. We breathe everyday until we take our last breath and then we don't breathe anymore. With that last breath, our body, deprived of oxygen (and the life force), has lost its support system. It dies.

"Improper breathing is a common cause of ill health."
—Andrew Weil, M.D.

Are you ready to take charge of your breathing, your body, your mind?

BREATH AND THE BODY

This is not the first lesson in *The 52* that has been devoted to the breath. How we breathe is so important that many of us spend a lifetime learning the subtle nature of the breath. The more we know about it, the more we observe how its functioning alters our health, how we think and how we feel.

Take the body first: If you asked most people, they would tell you that they want a strong and healthy body, one that will take them throughout their lives without illness. We may say this but do we do what is needed? Setting aside the obvious—those who smoke or use their nose to knowingly inhale toxic substances—we forget that disease has a step up in a body deprived of oxygen. Of course we know about lung diseases, but what about cell deprivation in all the cells of your body? What if you never fully breathe? What if you breathe the wrong way? What if you voluntarily stop breathing as a habit?

Does the health of your body matter enough to you to spend a little time learning to breathe?

You can learn to improve your breathing. Try this:

- Are you breathing all the way down into your belly? Or is your breath up there, high in the chest? Consciously, make yourself breathe more deeply, into the belly.
- Is the breath fast and choppy instead of slow and steady? You want it to be long and smooth. Work on it!
- Do you stop breathing? When you do certain things or think certain thoughts or move your body certain ways?

When you are angry or afraid? Don't stop breathing! Keep it going. When you hold your breath you deprive it of oxygen and throw off the rhythm. Maybe you are holding off your life.

- Don't just check your breathing once or twice a day. Do it a lot. Give yourself some kind of reminder, a signal, something you see or hear and, each time you are reminded to check your breath. It isn't a chore and won't take much time. Just do it!
- Each time you breathe, take it as a blessing. Breathe in love, clarity, good health, kindness, and breathe out illness, weakness, anger, or anything you want removed.

My favorite poet, the Sufi master of Divine Love, Rumi, wrote:

"There is a way of breathing that's a shame and a suffocation
And there's a way of expiring, a love breath,
That lets you open infinitely."

What about you? Would you like your simple breathing to change the quality of your life? You have the power, you know! It is so easy.

"For breath is life.
If you breathe well, you live long on earth."

This quote is said to be a Sanskrit proverb. I would add to it, not only might you live long on earth, the quality of that time will be greatly enhanced. You can do this by learning from your breath and by being a student of breathing.

I remember in my yoga teacher training with some of the most prominent thinkers on breathing as my teachers, I was quite taken by this expression:

If you can control your breath, you can control your life.

Ponder the meaning of these words. It is a life changing statement. I was both in wonder of it, the first time I heard it, and skeptical as to the enormity of the claim. By controlling my breath, I could control my life? How was that possible? Now I know it be true.

This is what I have learned:

- When I am conscious of my breathing—using proper diaphragmatic inhalation and exhalation in a steady, smooth stream—both my body and my mind grow calm.
- Focusing on breathing, rather than outside influences, draws me inward and into the core of my own place of Divine Light and Love.
- Visualizing the inhalation and exhalation as healing and spreading healing and calm within me and all around me causes a shift in my perceptions of the world.
- Being aware that I am subject to the events around me, which may evoke stress or fear, I can remember to go straight to the breath to shut down the fight/flight mode.

I don't say that I am perfect at this. Of course, I sometimes forget and falter. But when I do, I don't waste time berating myself or feeling guilty that I dropped my guard. I just go on.

The poet, Elizabeth Barrett Browning, wrote this:

> *"He lives most life whoever breathes most air."*

Simple and to the point.

Now how are YOU breathing?

Lesson 33

HOW DO YOU
USE YOUR ENERGY?

We are vibrating bundles of energy! Our bodies. Our breath. Our thoughts. All that is around us. All that ever was. No wonder we are interconnected, at the primary level of being!

Energy is a precious thing. It is not just what propels us in our activities, providing the stamina needed to function in everyday life. Energy is everything! Literally! It is EVERYTHING! What does this mean to you and your life?

Do we seek to soar like the blue butterfly toward the light? Do we want to experience the bliss of knowing Divine Light and Love? Do we want to just plain be happier in our lives? If so, then we must become acutely aware of the energy in ourselves and in everything around us. We will learn that we feel different—better—when that energy feels pure and clear. Do you ever think about your own thoughts and actions and how they are affecting your energy (positive or negative) at that moment?

One way to understand this better is to look at the *yama,* in Sanskrit called *brahmacharya.* As you may recall, we have been exploring some of the guidelines laid out as the *yamas* in one of the most important books on yoga called *The Yoga Sutras.* Endeavoring to follow these guidelines can lead us to living a happier, lighter and more loving life. Conserving our energy through non-excess and through viewing all of life as sacred keeps our energy pure and powerful. *Brahmacharya* means "walking with God."

Brahmacharya—Pure in Energy

While this *yama* has often been described as indicating self-imposed celibacy and monastic living, it is far more complex than this. It was thought that retaining sexual energy would allow for greater energy in spiritual seeking, and this is likely true. But we live in an era different from that when it was quite usual for those on the spiritual path, (mostly males at the time and residing in India) to join monasteries for all of or portions of their adulthood. It is not my purpose in writing to delve deeply into the subject of energy only on this level. Suffice it to say that non-excess is of value in whatever we pursue. Yet there are profound lessons to be learned beyond this.

Every thought and act is a movement of energy. What choices do you make, every day, to keep your own energy pure and loving and to avoid excess?

Just recently, someone suggested I watch a new television series, praising the acting and writing. While I rarely watch television, I watched part of one episode. The characters were cruel, insensitive, and distasteful. The story line was dark and rife with violence, abuse, and double-dealing. It was, in short, repugnant to me. Why would I want to spend any time watching a program with this kind of energy? But most people think nothing of such leisure activities, as if they have no impact on them.

Here are some ways to observe how you use your energy:

- Do you deplete your energy in pursuits that are negative—like gossiping or listening to music that is caustic or viewing films that glorify ego and destructive behavior or reading stories (even the news) that are unceasingly unsettling?
- When observing mistreatment of others, do you join in? Do you bully just to be accepted?
- Do you sometimes find that you over-do—in eating, exercising, drinking, fulfilling your bucket list?
- If you can choose activities in your free time that feel good—like taking a walk in the woods or sitting and meditating or cooking a lovingly prepared nutritious meal or calling a sick friend—do you think about how fulfilling and boosting it will be to your own well-being?
- Trust your own truth. On some level you will know if what you are doing or thinking is depleting or diminishing your energy. Go with what enhances love and light.

These are simple ideas, but we often are paying no attention. We just operate by rote. "Oh, I always watch that news show or TV series." Stop! Pay attention! What you are doing is having an affect—on you and on everything around you.

Lesson 34

LOVE IS DIVINE
AND BEYOND REASON

"It is love that gives worth to all things."

These are the words of Saint Teresa of Avila, the Spanish mystic and Carmelite nun who lived in the 1500s. They are words of perennial wisdom and deserve attention in any era.

When I was growing up, there was not a lot of talk about love and what it was, what it meant. It was never clearly defined. No one in our family openly expressed loving each other, at least not in those words. Maybe it was just assumed. Our family was quite stoic and of Northern European heritage; the adults were more the silent type. Now, I understand this fully well through adult eyes. In those days, while I may have felt a commonality, an affection and sense of caring with much that was around me, it would never have occurred to me that I loved all of this. Or myself either, for that matter.

What about you? Did you grow up with people expressing feelings of love all around you? If you did, I think that is a fortunate thing. Some of my history may explain why I so openly and fervently now express feelings of love. It is liberating and feels so good. Why not spread it all around?

The great Sufi poet/saint, Rumi, wrote that

"Reason is powerless in the expression of love."

It seemed to me, in those days, that reason was the ONLY way I could get answers and figure out something as confusing as love. I looked to books and minds greater than my own to define love. When I read what Erich Fromm, the German social psychologist said in his book *The Art of Loving,* that if love between people was to be successful, it required these elements: care, responsibility, respect, and knowledge (which I can still recite by memory). I thought that was it! I failed to consider that the answer to my question was readily available in spiritual literature and in so many places outside of the scientific, rational, material world. I wasted a lot of time, (if time is a notion to be considered), spinning my wheels and suffering in the process.

Rumi also wrote this:

"If love is in your heart, you will find your way home."

It is no wonder then, that when I naively walked into Rumi's resting place, his shrine in Konya, Turkey, that I got a blast of energy so profound it brought me to tears. I did not have a clue who he was and what was happening, but I knew they were tears of joy, happiness and love. I needed to be dissolved in love, if only temporarily to know what this kind of love was like. Rumi gave me the experience of Divine Love, one of many that would follow by multiple sources. There was no going back. It was a turning point, as were many of the new mystical experiences that were unfolding around me. Unbeknownst to me, I was transitioning into a *bhakti yogi,* one whose path is love. And this was after all those years in study, as a *jnana yogi,* one who relied more on the mind. I had been relying on the head and mind for nice, neat rational answers when all along there they were—in my heart. But in truth, while yoga opened this door for me, it could have arisen from many other sources— from Christianity or Judaism or Islam or a myriad of other forms—I was ready to be bathed in love.

Now I am steeped in this love. At the core of my being, it is the only thing that matters and is authentic. I have been blessed with many teachers along the way. They arose from unexpected places, like the signs and messages and manifestations my mother sent to me after she departed the world. She was the perfect messenger to deliver the message that love is eternal. After all, she was not in this world any more, so there was something eternal going on. Then, as if by chance, another teacher just happened to arrive in my life.

My husband and I attended a Fourth of July garden luncheon at the home of dear friends. When we arrived, our hostess told me there was someone there I should meet, that we were both spiritual. As my new acquaintance and I sat at a table in the shade, surrounded by flowering gardens, she told me instantly that her belief was in Divine Light and Love. I don't know about you, but this is not a frequent topic of conversation at most country garden parties. I felt as if I had met an old friend, a kindred spirit. We understood one another in seconds. What grace, I thought. I felt intense gratitude. It was love at first sight—this expression of universal Love.

Ralph Waldo Emerson wrote this:

"Every man is divinity in disguise, a god playing the fool."

You never know how or when there will be a moment of enlightenment, when a spark of Love will be ignited that will alter your perception of everything in your life. It could be someone you meet, a phrase you read in a book, a quote on Facebook, a sign from someone departed, a scene in a movie, a sunset, a porpoise swimming next to your boat. It could be anything! But your senses must be open for it. Here are some ideas:

- When you meet someone, in any circumstance, try imagining that you are looking at a soul rather than just another person. See them through eyes of Love.
- Take a few moments, or as long as you can, to experience everything around as infused with love. Make that the words you are reading now, the chair where you are sitting, the device you are using to read this, the clothes you are wearing—everything. Then do this practice several times a day.
- Soften your present, past and future with feelings of love and acceptance. Set aside your normal mind based reactions. You can go back to them whenever you want.
- Now see yourself sitting in a pool of Divine Light, surrounded by Love. Say to yourself: I love myself completely NOW, then spread that love out to the space around you. This, by the way, is not very different from circumstances described by those who have near death experiences. They feel complete and total unconditional love. You can do this while in this life. You don't have to nearly die to know it.

I hope you will give serious attention to this subject of love.

You see, I know who you are. You may be in disguise, but I know who you are!

Lesson 35

SIMPLIFY YOUR LIFE
WITH APARIGRAHA

Aparigraha

Never heard of this word? Unless you are a student of yoga, that is likely so. Yet, as one of the many layers or limbs we study to bring our life into a place of peace—something classic yoga does very well—it is an extraordinary practice to know.

Aparigraha is a Sanskrit word that is defined as non-possessiveness. Grouped with the many other *yamas* which we have thus far explored, it is meant to guide us as we live in the world, in our bodies, surrounded by so much that we might desire. If you look back at the previous posts on the *yamas,* you will see that there is symmetry within them. They work hand in hand to offer points of wisdom. With all the many objects and experiences that seem to reach out to us, from all directions, it is a relief to know how to let go of them.

Bear in mind that this does not mean that the goal is to live in a cave, without possessions, engulfed in full-time meditation (which some, in fact, do choose). It means to live in a non-grasping, greedless, non attached state. We can certainly enjoy all the benefits that the world offers yet remain apart from them and not needing them to define us.

Non-Possessiveness

The renowned yoga master and teacher, B.K.S Iyengar, wrote this:

*"By the observance of aparigraha,
the yogi makes his life as simple as possible
and trains his mind not to feel the loss or lack of anything.
Then everything he needs is welcome
to him by itself at the proper time."*

I admit that this is a practice that has posed great challenges for me. While it is easy for me to be mostly detached from items of luxury and status, many times in my life I have been attached to experiences like traveling all around the world, sampling the foods from the most new and trendy restaurants, developing a familiarity with the arts on many levels—going to museums and symphonies and films. It took a long time for me to recognize that I was chasing my tail. There would always be another exotic location to see, another restaurant to try, another movie to view. I slowly began to recognize how futile it was to keep trying to be in the know.

But that is not all! I do not part easily with memorabilia. I have yet to clean out all those boxes in my attic, even though I have not looked in many of them for years. I am a perfect candidate for taking a course in simplicity of possessions. And books are my greatest attachment! I need to wear blinders when I walk into a bookstore. At least I can see some humor in these traits and do not ever use this as a means for self-criticism. All that stuff is there, and I tell myself, I live in simple ways on other levels.

As I believe that everything is part of Divine Consciousness, even those musty boxes, and that everything unfolds with purpose and at just the right time, I take it easy on myself. Enjoying my life without attachment, I say.

So I write these words for myself:

- What are you capable of releasing and letting go? What would happen if you did not own this or did not do that?
- Can you fully appreciate and care deeply for what you have in your life, while packing lightly?
- Is it possible to imagine how much freedom you have when you are not in the throws of desires and perceived needs?
- Try this: When you are on the verge of something to purchase, take a few breaths and see if the desire (which may be emanating from the ego) will begin to detach.
- Do you know when you are clinging to something?
- Finally, whatever your answers on all of this, it matters that you still experience kindness and unconditional love for yourself. Always!

This is really all about letting our lives become more simple and peaceful and learning how to truly enjoy what we have in a way that shines with the Light of Truth.

Now I think I better start unpacking those boxes in the attic today.

But wait! There is time tomorrow...

Lesson 36

BE STILL AND REMEMBER
WHO YOU ARE!

Are you afraid to be quiet? Is it too daunting to think of being alone with yourself? What will happen if you turn off the
sounds around you—the iPod, the radio, the TV, the chatting on
the phone, the texting—all that surrounds you? Or maybe, wise
you, you don't live in this kind of noise any more.

Are we so addicted to all this noisy input that we cannot fathom
what it is like to see how it feels to be quiet? Maybe we have
become what James Thurber, the great humorist, suggested:

> *"Nowadays most men live lives of noisy desperation."*

BE STILL

Several years ago, when we were living in a quiet, leafy suburb
of Chicago, we invited a successful playwright/college friend to
stay with us as one of his plays was being produced in Chicago.
He lived in the heart of New York City in an apartment surrounded by bustling activity and noise. After a few hours,

sitting on the veranda at our home, with birds chirping, leaves gently rustling in the breeze, and squirrels making their way from one branch to another, he could not stand it any longer. He blurted out, "How can you stand it here? It is too quiet!" My husband and I were so stunned that we laughed in response.

> *"The Arctic expresses the sum of all wisdom: silence."*
> —Walter Bauer

Well, most of us will not be going to the Arctic anytime soon. So what about you? Can you stand a little silence? I don't mean meditating, though that would be even better. I only suggest being still and turning off the outside chatter. You might even choose to go somewhere that is relatively quiet—somewhere like a path in the woods or a park or to a museum or library. In these places you will still have nature and artworks and books to keep you company, but at least the noise will be less. You might at some point realize that you (yes, you) are pretty good company to keep. And then your chattering mind might find it pleasant to drop back and relax.

Here are some ideas:
- Actively notice when you are bombarded with auditory influences and sound, then take note of times when you let these go. How does it feel?
- Make a conscious effort to take a little time each day to shut out exterior sound. Don't try to find another distraction, like reading or texting. Just be.
- Make those times longer. Perhaps set a time aside to be still and each day make it a priority.
- You might make it even more positive by adding a statement. At the beginning of your quiet time say, "I love myself completely NOW." Or, "I enjoy this time to myself." Or any phrase that makes you feel good.

- As time goes on, you may notice that you can be silent, calm and peaceful, even when surrounded by blaring sounds and cacophony.

This idea of stillness did not always come easy to me, so I can sympathize if this seems hard. Recently I went to a spiritual retreat center, a kind of summer camp for seekers. At dinner I looked for a table marked with a sign that read "silence." Most ashrams and places of this sort have them, so I was disappointed that there was no table to just sit and feel the pleasure of nourishing good food.

On the reverse, long ago, I was at a social gathering with a group of loquacious, high energy TV producers and others. Someone had heard of experiments on being silent. We agreed to try it and see how long we could be together without talking. It lasted for a while, with none of us used to such a thing. And guess who was the first to break the silence, to feel compelled to make some joke? That's right. I could not just relax with the quiet.

Now there is little I relish more than stillness, my mantra and meditation. Just being, that's all.

Mother Teresa made this statement:

> *"We need to find God and he cannot*
> *be found in noise and restlessness.*
> *God is the friend of silence.*
> *See how nature—trees, flowers, grass—grows in silence.*
> *See the stars, the moon, the sun, how they move in silence...*
> *We need silence in order to touch souls."*

Who knows? In silence you may touch your own soul—and God.

Lesson 37

FORGIVENESS IS DIVINE

Do you hold grudges? Do you let resentment and hatred surge through your being? Do you think that forgiveness implies weakness and steals from you the right to be indignant, furious, and angry? Are you proud of your capacity to punish someone by banishing them from your midst or by spreading terrible words about them? Did it ever occur to you that the one most hurt by all of this is you? That you are drinking the poison and expecting someone else to die? Is it possible that lack of forgiveness is really a sign of fear?

It was Alexander Pope who wrote:

"To err is human, to forgive divine."

Aren't we all human? Don't we all make mistakes? Haven't we all stumbled and failed at some time in our lives? Isn't there some dark shadow of guilt or shame lurking in the recesses of our lives? Is it too radical to consider these possibilities: From the depth of love that resounds in our hearts, we can—and must—forgive others. And coupled with that, we can—and must—forgive ourselves. What will be the outcome? Freedom! True freedom. And a kind of salvation, too.

Can we be forgiving about our own times of lack of forgiveness? Are we big enough, strong enough, powerful and loving enough to choose forgiveness? That is the focus of this lesson.

Forgiving Sets Us Free

A Course in Miracles is an awe-inspiring book that has the capacity to transform anyone who follows the course. (Studying it has been one of the most pivotal experiences and best decisions of my life.) I am so devoted to this book that I offer Study Groups to follow the daily lessons and discuss the profound wisdom found within its pages. In the first years I spent reading and imbibing the Course, I found myself completely at ease with the belief system; though offered from a slightly different perspective, the Truths were the same as those I had long studied in the ancient texts of yoga. Forgiveness is a key theme.

> *Fear binds the world. Forgiveness sets it free.*
> —Lesson 332 *A Course in Miracles*

Imagine what your life and world would be like if you shed the burdens you have carried by refusing to forgive. We, as humans, have carried so many foolish notions on this subject. Not long ago, someone was telling me about a woman who was generally kind and loving, but "if you crossed her once, she never forgave you." This was told to me with a hint of admiration for the woman who never forgave, as if she had some stupendous power, like a Mafia Don, as if it was a sign of merit and strong character. One mistake with her and—BOOM—banished forever.

I wonder if she would have ever considered these words from George Herbert:

"He who cannot forgive breaks the bridge
over which he himself must pass."

Forgiveness must go in all directions, passing through all relationships, into what we perceive as the past and the future, from one generation to another and globally as well. I think of the damage done to families that have held onto angers, like the Hatfields and the McCoys. This brings to mind political stances, like Democrats never forgiving the Republican politicians for something or other (you can reverse the party title for the same effect) or citizens of one country bearing the blame for sins committed long before they were born, such as longstanding anger with anyone from the Mideast or Europe or the United States or, go ahead, fill in the blank.

If we are to wipe the slate clean, it has to start somewhere. How about starting it yourself, with you?

Now take a calming few breaths, quiet your mind and try some or all of these ideas:

- Are you aware of a long-standing anger you have harbored for someone? Or maybe it is a surge of anger that started just yesterday? Can you actually see that person through a lens of forgiveness, trying to fathom who they are and what it may feel like in their shoes for a minute or so?
- Can you entertain the possibility that you are harming, not them, but yourself by holding onto these emotions? That actual physical symptoms, like high blood pressure or depression, may be a result of lack of forgiveness.

- If it helps you can always write a letter, which you will not send, to the person who has wronged you. Get it off your chest (notice what this phrase means with regard to your heart), whatever has to be said. Then let it go!
- Can you dig into your past and find the place where you began to believe you were unworthy, unlovable and unforgivable? Can you look at it now, see that the past is over, and let light merge into that spot? You might visualize the "you" from the past and send love, saying "I love myself completely NOW," to that person you were then.
- Try seeing your long perceived enemy in the same light. Aren't we all just doing the best we can to get through life? Aren't we all capable of mistakes? What if you chose to spread Love instead? Do you think this is all silly and a waste of time? Have you ever tried it? How about setting the ego aside for a little while and making a new choice? You can do it, you know.
- Be patient and kind with yourself. This way of forgiveness may not become a habit overnight. It may take a little practice. Give it some time and see how you feel. Remember to keep loving yourself all the time.

Here is a quote attributed to Mark Twain, the legendary American author and humorist. I think it expresses a profundity beyond measure.

"Forgiveness is the fragrance the violet sheds
on the heel that has crushed it."

Lesson 38

WELL, JUST HOW PURE ARE YOU?

What a challenge! Can we be pure in body, mind, spirit, thoughts, and words? What if you think you have accomplished one of them and then you have a little slip? Say, you eat only raw foods, but you go to a banquet and eat something else? Or you promise yourself you will only have pure thoughts, and then anger arises? What then? Is it time to go back to the last lesson—on forgiveness?

Purification is spoken about in many spiritual disciplines. In yoga it is called, in Sanskrit, *saucha,* and refers to purification on many levels—in body, mind and heart, in thought and action. *Saucha* is the first of the *niyamas* or observances that make up a part of the *Yoga Sutras,* the comprehensive and reliable path as laid out by the yoga sage, Patanjali. This eight-fold or eight-limbed guide is thoughtful and as relevant today as it was at the time it was written. I like to think of *sutras* as guidelines. If we are too rigid, we (and the ego) might use them as a means to beat ourselves up, to judge ourselves and others. From my viewpoint, that would defeat the whole idea that we are loved unconditionally, right now, just as we are.

Saucha—Purity

When I was fairly new to yoga and its teachings, I took very seriously the idea of purification of the body. I was learning to be a teacher of hatha yoga and understood very well how two of the limbs of classic yoga were effective for the body— *asana* (the postures or poses of yoga), and *pranayama* (breath work). Simply expressed, the poses are effective in purifying the physical body as well as the energy system, the *nadis* and the *chakras*. The breathing practices help cleanse and purify by moving oxygen and *prana* through the body. Of course, the mind and spirit benefit as well.

In addition to these forms of purification, there were others that I embraced. They were things like weekly fasting on water and juices, cleansing through daily use of a neti pot and sending water through and out both nostrils, eye *asanas* to clear the eyes, and various and sundry other cleansings. I can still hear the gasps from my yoga students when I described the method of fasting and induced vomiting to empty the stomach of mucus and old contents (we call it seasonal purging.) Well, let's just say, without going into even more shocking methods, you could spend a lot of time on cleansing the body. I sure felt clean, but I'm not sure I was doing the big time, real purifications I needed—like purifying the mind and thought and heart.

Of course, I tended to want pure and fresh foods, eaten with intention and reverence. My diet styles shifted and changed. I had jars of sprouts growing; I ground my flax seeds and balanced non-animal proteins and felt quite virtuous and a little smug, too. Wasn't I just being so pure? In point of fact, wasn't I just deceiving myself? Every morning, before I began my formal meditation, my mind wandered through all the *yamas* and *niyamas,* giving myself a kind of check list of how I was faring on the spiritual path of yoga. Did I notice that while I thought I scored high on some measures, I still lacked forgiveness? I was harsh in my judgment of others and myself. I didn't understand the subtleties of these concepts. I had a long way to go.

Only when the purification really began to happen in my mind and heart, in actions and thoughts, did I know for sure that I was actually doing something transformational.

Here are a few ideas to consider. For some they are baby steps. For others, they may be old hat. It never hurts to be a beginner again.

- Look at your body. Is there something you can do today to help to purify and nurture your body? Maybe you will drink some glasses of pure clean water or have a cup of green tea. Perhaps you will do some yoga stretches or take a walk outside. How about not eating that hot dog loaded with additives? You may wish to speak to your body about how much you appreciate it. Whatever you choose, let it be filled with love and pleasure.
- Try changing your attitude towards something that is routine, like vacuuming the rug or taking out the trash. Think of it as purifying and cleansing. Imbue it with positive energy. Cleaning out a closet could be like this. Or taking away clothing you no longer wear and giving it to others who would appreciate those garments.
- Take a moment to see how you are thinking. Is it time to clean out the closet of your thoughts? Like getting rid of complaining and negativity, judging and arguing. You might even consider a little silence, giving your mind a chance to rest and be quiet. Or you could meditate for a bit of time or extend your meditation.

Ultimately, the following are the words I like best. I could not find the attribution, so I am not sure who made this point, but, nonetheless:

"The only 'dirt' is Avidya, ignorance of the True Self."

When you know who you are and that you are Divine Light and Love, your heart sings and everything else is window dressing.

Lesson 39

MANY PATHS TO TRUTH, WHAT IS YOURS?

Henry David Thoreau wrote:

> *"Pursue some path, however narrow and crooked,*
> *in which you can walk with love and reverence."*

Over the years I followed many paths, though I am not sure I always knew what I was seeking. There was the path of my childhood Christian faith, then the path of rebellion when I disavowed all that was religious or spiritual. Even so, I was pulled toward discussions about God, either positive or negative. Then something happened, and I went in a different direction. My journey has seen me forge ahead on a variety of paths, but they were all leading to one place—to Truth, Realization, Eternal and Divine Love, and to God. While yoga and the ancient texts, so resonant with wisdom, opened the first doors and still are the mainstay of my understandings, Buddhism, Christianity, Sufism, and just about any system that is heart-led are now my passion.

What about you? Have you seen take-aways and "aha" moments in writings that emerge from a source different from some spiritual path you have followed?

THE PATHS TO TRUTH

"Many are stubborn in the pursuit of the path
they have chosen, few in pursuit of the goal."
—Friedrich Nietzsche

You've met them. We all have. People who embrace a belief system, then fight (sometimes to the death) in serving that path, even when they seem clueless about reaching the goal of Truth and what it is. We might call this blind faith. And in many ways it is a dangerous thing. It is a sort of fundamentalism that stretches across the spectrum of religions, but it also may be planted deeply in non-theistic thought, like atheism, or political correctness. It hinges on the belief that the believer is superior to others who disagree. It loses touch with the common and more important themes of forgiveness, love, compassion, and non-duality.

I have had quite a learning curve in understanding what it means to know Truth. I will never forget being with my friend who introduced me to the Siddha Path of Yoga and the guru system. I was too naive then to understand that she was there as a teacher and guide, and some might say, an angel for me. One day, after she had visited me in my home, I drove her to a car rental. As she got into the car to continue her journey, she waved to me with a broad smile and said, "I intend to become fully realized in this lifetime." I raised my hand to bid her adieu as her words engulfed me and a kind of astonishment began to sink in. In my child's mind (spiritually speaking), it never occurred to me that someone would actually become enlightened now, in this life. Didn't that take lifetimes? Weren't we far from the mark? Weren't we too imperfect? How could this be?

This was before I understood that we are already realized and we just don't know it a lot of the time, if ever. That we are already the Light of Love and God. That we have always been that and always will be that. That when we understand and trust that we are in the loving arms of Grace or the guru or Christ or Buddha or God, that we can relax and be guided. That most of us think this world, this material place with all it sensory input, IS the whole deal. But that is not what we as eternal beings believe. We are, in fact, already perfect. Yes, I said PERFECT.

I came to see that all the subsequent paths I walked, in tandem with my early Christian and yoga studies, pointed to the same thing. It might have been the writings of Rumi or years of study in *A Course in Miracles* or The Sedona Method and many others. The veil was parting, the Truth was emerging, the wonder was abundant, and mystical events were unfolding all around me. Nothing would ever be the same again!

These are some questions to consider:

- Does the path you follow lead to forgiveness, love, acceptance, and kindness for all beings?
- Whatever your belief system, do you know that you are unconditionally loved at all times?
- Do you feel empowered by your path or diminished, not quite good enough, because of it?
- Are you happy and fulfilled on your journey?
- Does fear play any part in the belief system you follow? If so, does this feel comfortable for you?
- Do you love and accept yourself completely on this path?

It is not my role or my goal to try to persuade you to join a certain path. Everyone has free choice and can make this decision on their own. I only hope that you will consider the possibility that this world is not all there is in life. You could find that going within is be far superior to projecting outward. You might be "looking for love in all the wrong places" when it is already right there, within you!

There are so many paths leading to Love. I hope you will choose one, open your heart, and experience ecstatic joy.

Lesson 40

CAN YOU REST IN CONTENTMENT?

"Once you have tasted contentment and start to live in its
beauty, you actually want this river to overflow its banks.
And that gives you the courage to move forward
and make the most of this gift of life."

—Gurumayi Chidvilasananda

Someone in one of my yoga classes visually blanched when I
mentioned the idea of contentment. "But if we are content," she
exclaimed, "then we won't strive to improve. We won't make
an effort. We won't grow and learn. We will just be content."
Exactly! We will just be content. But this doesn't mean we become a bump on a log, that we are inert and lacking in vitality.
It means something far more important. It means this: If you
start from a place of contentment with what is in the moment,
you move forward without a sense of lack. You are conscious of
your value and worth as you move in whatever direction you
might go.

How content are you right now? Can you rest in the place where
you are in this moment? Or do you feel lacking, desiring, and

inadequate without this and that? As part of this 52 week study, we are moving through the Yoga Sutras. They contain enormous wisdom and are guides to aid us in everyday life. One of the *Niyamas* is called *santosha* or contentment in English. These are guideposts for living our lives in ways that direct us toward lightness and happiness and greater self-knowledge and, ultimately, to the great Light and Love that lives in each of us—to the Divine Self.

Contentment—Santosha

There was a time in my life when the idea of contentment would have been anathema to me. I had so many lists of goals and plans and desires—from books I wanted to read, to destinations around the world where I wanted to travel, to languages I hoped I might learn to speak, and, well, blah, blah, blah, and on and on *ad infinitum*. My tape deck in my car was full of ways to change my life, wasting no time while I drove from one location to another— listening to lessons on how to improve myself, repeating French phrases or German or Chinese, learning something or other. I set up the perfect arrangement to never, ever feel content and finished in this lifetime and probably for many to come. And worst of all, I felt pride in my list making and goal setting, stupidly thinking that people who were content were lazy and lacked vision. In the meantime, I was dancing as fast as I could, and never happy or fulfilled. There was always more to add to the list.

Now I know better.

The *Yoga Vasishtha* is an ancient document which contains many of my favorite writings. It says:

"What is contentment? To renounce all cravings for what is not obtained unsought and to be satisfied with what comes unsought. Without being elated or depressed even by them — this is contentment."

Think about it. Are you always looking outside yourself for something to bring you peace and contentment? To something you want? To another person to accept and provide a sense of worth? Seeking and avoiding—that is no way to feel fulfilled and content. Ask me! I have been an expert at this. And I know what it brought me. Here is what I got: nothing but pain, sadness, arrogance, depression, and helplessness.

Now here are some ideas that might be helpful:

- Stop. Right now. In this moment. Stop reading. Are you content just sitting and reading? Is this possible? Maybe, in this moment, even if only for a fraction of time, you are content. Don't ask for more right now. How does this feel to you?
- Do you really think that once you have that new BMW or that trip around the world or that book published or that retirement fund built up, that this will ensure contentment? Are you looking outside yourself?
- Can you begin to imagine that there is already a treasure of wisdom that outranks everything "out there" residing right there, in you? Just knowing that you are worthy and loved without all the *accoutrements*, the add-ons from the world, is quite a gift.
- Could you let go of desire and know that everything will unfold perfectly anyway, without your own effort?

Leading from a place of contentment opens up a whole new world. But first you have to try it and then stay with it.

"Through contentment, there is a world within my heart."
—Rumi

Lesson 41

YOU TRAVEL BUT IN DREAMS
WHILE SAFE AT HOME

"There are more things in heaven and earth,
Horatio, than are dreamt of in your philosophy."
—William Shakespeare

Do you remember the last time you had a vivid dream and when you awakened from it, you said this to yourself." Oh, thank God that was just a dream." You were relieved that what had seemed so completely real, so true while you were dreaming, what troubled or frightened you, was not real at all. You were dreaming it and now, no longer sleeping, you can take solace in knowing that it was all illusion. How many times has this happened to you? For me, it is more times than I could ever count.

But here is another thought. What if this happens? You are at your moment of death, perhaps on your deathbed, you breathe the last breath of your life, and now, according to the measurements we use to designate when someone has officially died, you are technically dead. That's how it appears to the world, but something else happens to you. Something you might not have expected, maybe even something outside of whatever belief system you may have embraced in life. Instead of dropping into nothingness, into a dark blankness, a void, you actually wake up. This time you REALLY wake up into a reality bigger and better than anything you could have conceived. You wake up to Eternal Life and Love. You have never felt more alive and joyous. You say to yourself, "Oh my, all of that stuff before this was only a dream." Maybe what you took to be your life all those years was only a dream.

You have just been introduced to *maya,* the Sanskrit word that denotes illusion or "that which is not."

It is not surprising that I have waited until the last lessons to introduce this idea. For most of us it is too radical, too crazy, too impossible to consider. We are taught to believe that the only reality is the one we think of as the material, left brain, Newtonian universe. We often cling to this belief, yet there is much to the contrary. There is much that is not explainable by science and the experiences of the five senses. But now, even science is beginning to find truth in these ancient beliefs written thousands of years ago by enlightened beings.

I believe this to the core of my being: the world as we experience it is nothing more than *maya,* an illusion beyond time and space. And yet, ironically, embracing this allows us to love without conditions and to witness ourselves with acceptance in this "play," this life on the stage of *maya.*

Maya—The Illusion

I am fully aware that this topic, this lesson, will feel totally implausible to many of you. It surely did to me when I first heard of it. Illusion? More like delusion, I thought. If you already discount near death experiences, after death communications, communication with other realms, and the credible information shared by many hospice workers, then this will be a stretch. And if you believe that all the spiritual writings of antiquity and today, as well as belief systems in many religions are all bunk, then you have probably already stopped reading this. I get it! I used to share your incredulity, I was just like you. I changed. And you are welcome to come along or not. No matter.

If you happen to be steeped in science, it might interest you to know that great physicists like Einstein, Niels Bohr, Steven Hawking, and David Bohm have weighed in with the findings of quantum physics. Who would have thought that science is coming around, at last, to the ideas that were conveyed thousands of years ago in spiritual texts? How about this? The physical world that most people take to be real and solid is nothing more than illusion. Or this? Space and time and causality are purely mental bonds. We created all this ourselves.

It was not, by the way, a typo in the title of this lesson. I meant to write hOMe. The sound "om" from which we derive Shalom, Salaam, Amen, and home is thought to have infinite power within it. Some say it is the sound of all creation that resonates in each of us, as a memory somewhere in our consciousness. When my mother was near death, she, who was not overtly a particularly religious person, exclaimed out loud and to no one I could see, "home soon." She seemed to be talking to someone in her bedroom. I was stunned at her words. She knew she was going "home." She looked radiant when she said it.

> *"You dwell not here but in eternity.*
> *You travel but in dreams, while safe at home."*
> *—A Course in Miracles*

While I will write more on this subject in the future, I hope you will consider this:

- What if you felt safe and at home even in the midst of world events, problems, illness? In the midst of the illusion.
- Could you take a few moments to be quiet and consider that all is unfolding in your "play" in a way that you may not understand right now, but that it means something?
- Can you entertain the notion or even consider the potential that the material world is not all there is? Could you imagine that what seems to have "form" or is material is a projection of your mind? Would it be possible to envision something more transcendent than all of this around you?
- Could you stand aside, even for moments, to become a witness to yourself and everything around you? Would it all still be there without any sensory acknowledgement of it?
- Could you learn to view the illusion in all its grandness and beauty and awesomeness as something to be enjoyed even while knowing it is a play?
- Maybe consciousness is all there is. How about that?

I wish you *bon voyage* on your journey beyond the dream and into Truth. There is nothing more exciting, and it is all in your own loving heart.

Lesson 42

DO YOU INCLUDE YOURSELF IN COMPASSIONATE THINKING?

"If your compassion doesn't include yourself, it is incomplete."
—Jack Kornfield

What about you? Can you be sensitive, caring, and extend kindnesses to others while ignoring yourself completely? Are you able to look with understanding on the failings and sad situations of others in their struggles, yet hold back the same level of compassion for yourself? It seems that some of us buy into the notion that expressing compassion for ourselves is egotistical and inappropriate. How dare we make the same allowances for ourselves as we might convey to others!

Compassion must begin at home, in us. If we do not consider ourselves worthy and deserving of this self-care, then how can we legitimately pass it on to others? Compassion must grow from a sense of self-love and from our own open hearts.

COMPASSION

Compassion! I have written on many subjects that relate to this issue of compassion—kindness, forgiveness, gratitude, and love—but not directly focusing on compassion. Yet compassion, for others and for ourselves, offers us spiritual insights that the other topics do not. It engages a sense of empathy that allows us to enter into a special place with another. We walk in their shoes.

Can you, on a constant level, use the practice of compassion to alter how you see yourself and others in the world? Can you bring compassion into your awareness even at times when your anger has been activated and your impatience has risen too high? I have often found this to be a challenge. I can easily site chapter and verse when I lacked compassion for myself and for others. Until I learned to practice forgiveness in all ways, (which may not happen instantaneously as it is a process), I allowed myself to be tortured in this unhealthy state.

Maybe some of these suggestions will be helpful to you:

- Engage the silent witness practice which I have written about previously. Stand aside and look with compassion and great kindness on yourself, no matter what you have done in the present or past. See yourself through the eyes of one who is all forgiving and loving. It could be represented by a deity, an angel, a loving parent, a spirit guide, God, but ultimately it is you. It is always the heart connection within yourself.
- Look all around you—in the present and into the past. Are there other fellow human beings you have cut out of your circle of acceptance due to disagreements, political persuasion, class lines, or anything else? You can take a try at engaging acceptance and compassion by seeing them through impartial eyes or as they may see the

world. Aren't you doing more damage to yourself than to them by seeing yourself as superior or self-righteous in your attitude? Maybe those assessments are cover-ups for your own damaged self that could use some healing.

· Now take a moment to think about other cohabitants in the world—the animals, plants, and the whole of ecology. We humans have so often wantonly destroyed our own home, decimating animal populations and forests, for example. Everything is part of the same energy system. Just maybe that tree you chopped down and that deer you just shot is related to your own soul—especially if these acts were for personal gain and not necessity.

· Remember, as is the philosophy in *The 52,* that you use none of these lessons in such a way that you feel less loving to yourself. Everything unfolds with Divine Consciousness in this play of the world. Every practice you use is meant to increase the Love you feel for yourself.

As the Dalai Lama has observed:

"It is lack of love for ourselves that
inhibits our compassion towards others.
If we make friends with ourselves, then there is no obstacle to
opening our hearts and minds to others."

Whenever there is a choice, choose Love—for yourself and others. It is an easy choice and always the right one.

Lesson 43

Tapas: The Flame of Change

Tapas. Ah! Spanish food! But no, this is not the kind you eat at a Spanish restaurant—all those delicious small plates of food. But, in another way, this kind of tapas is food, too. It is food for your soul and your eternal being. In *tapas,* one might say we are "cooked" into something new. We are "cracked open" so a greater understanding can emerge.

Tapas is a Sanskrit word that describes yet another of the *niyamas,* the ethical practices as set out in classic yoga philosophy. It is a guideline to help us live in the world while still embracing the spiritual essence of our own being. Most of us are not monks or hermits, living apart from everyday life. We need systems of support along the way. Thus, we have the eight limbs of yoga. And, thus, we have *tapas.*

Tapas—The Flame of Change and Enthusiasm

The word, *tapas,* has been described in a variety of ways. Some say it is a fire that burns within and fosters wisdom, integrity, simplicity, and focus. Others laud its ability to trigger enthusiasm and excitement, pushing us ever more to release all distractions and bring us through the flames to a place of deep balance and tranquility. Others explain *tapas* as that which kindles the flame of the divine within us and burns away all impurities. All of these describe the richness that is *tapas*.

It is useful to think of the practice of *tapas* when we are in the midst of crisis, change, and pain. When it seems that some sort of catharsis is occurring and pressing us into a sometimes dramatic change. When something within us is being burned away so that a new version of ourselves may appear. For myself personally, a few years ago my path took me into a place of deep loss and fear. It was a falling away from what I thought I had been. Something new was struggling to make itself known—in effect, a new me. It felt like being burned up until, at last, I could see the debris was melted away, and I was glad to see it go.

> *"Your pain is the breaking of the shell*
> *that encloses your understanding."*
> —Khalil Gibran

Pain and loss are not uncommon in the physical world and while we are residing there, even in it as a dream, our feathers get ruffled. Or maybe we are shaken to the core of our being. At those times, staying steadfast in our beliefs is a powerful means of unearthing the pearl within the shell. Sometimes we become so immersed in this play of grief, self-pity, anger, and other emotions, that it is hard to catch the spiritual drift. Swami Muktananda wrote:

> *"The secret to success in sadhana* (spiritual practices) *is to use everything to our advantage."*

There are legions of stories about those who have turned tragedy into enlightened experiences. Take, for example, St. John of the Cross in his writings in *The Dark Night of the Soul.* His suffering carried him into the arms of the Divine. Or consider the response of Ram Dass, a contemporary teacher on the spiritual path who, much to his surprise, suffered a stroke some years ago, leaving him quite debilitated physically. Yet this experience of "fierce grace," as he called it, resulted in him naming his experience as "being stroked" by God.

Don't be mistaken, it is my wish that none of us are so blessed as to reach deep levels of pain, but perhaps we can begin to see that the fire that consumes the forest makes way for new shoots to spring from the soil. It is a form of rebirth that allows the Divine within each of us to shine in the light of day.

These ideas may help you better understand *tapas:*

- When you are confronted with levels of fear, pain, or loss, what might you do to ground yourself? Would it help for you to take a walk, listen to some music, do yoga poses, watch your breath, meditate, read a book that makes you laugh, go out and hug (literally) a tree, spend time with a supportive friend? What about praying, asking for guidance and strength? Or reading some passages that help you remember who you are?
- Using affirmations can bring a lift. Saying "I love myself completely NOW," can be helpful in giving something positive for the mind to give focus, and breaking a pattern of negative thinking.
- Can you remember times when you felt lost and afraid? Do you remember how long this lasted? Did something else arise to replace that experience? Can you recall in any way that those feelings and emotions were constantly changing, yet you, the real you, was still there, unchanging. Are you able to see that you made it through and came out stronger?

- Try thinking of ways that sustain you and keep you steady, when you are not in the eye of the storm. If you devote more to those habits, like eating good, healthy food, caring for your body, finding coping mechanisms for stress, taking time to go inward, laughing, giving love and forgiveness to yourself and others, they will be set in your everyday life. All of these build up strength for times of duress and flame the fires of joy and happiness within us.

Remember that *tapas* builds enthusiasm, and fires us up for confronting whatever may arrive in our lives. So let the multiple meanings of *tapas* enrich your life in new and surprising ways. We are all in this together walking hand in hand on the path that guides us to Eternal Love.

Lesson 44

I Was Just Thinking...

Stop! Right now! What have you been thinking? Do you even know?

Thoughts have power and energy within them. That's a fact. Some say, "As you think, so you become." Unfortunately, most of us just think the same old stuff over and over again, as if the mind runs by itself and has a mind of its own. It is on automatic pilot. THAT is a problem. While you are far more than your mind, it is your mind. So pay attention. That pesky mind, when it aligns with the ego, can do a lot of damage. It can end up defining you in ways you might not prefer.

I have written on this subject before. I urge you to go back and look at Lesson 16. It offers a valuable means of monitoring and changing thought patterns. Following that practice was life changing for me. It could do the same for you. Try it.

HOW THOUGHTS AFFECT WHO YOU THINK YOU ARE

Yoga and other spiritual paths are rich with words defining the mind. In fact, with regard to yoga, some would say understanding the mind and letting it go IS the definition of yoga. As Patanjali wrote in the *Yoga Sutras:*

"Yoga is cessation of the modifications of the mind."

And in the *Yoga Vasishtha:*

> *"The world is produced from the mind alone,*
> *like the waters of a mirage.*
> *It manifests in the form of fleeting thoughts,*
> *which are as illusory as the reflections of the moon on water."*

Without doubt, these are potent concepts and not likely to appeal to those new to them. So let's take smaller steps. I have written earlier on thought monitoring and learning to know what you think, then taking action to alter those thoughts. This time I will draw from a course I studied some years ago. It is called The Sedona Method. The man who developed it, Lester Levenson, was a highly successful and innovative physicist and entrepreneur in New York City. He was in such ill-health and, in effect, given a death sentence by his doctors. Instead of retreating and waiting to die, he found a means to help himself. Thus, he created the Sedona Method. Breaking it down into a nutshell does not do justice to his work, but here is a taste.

This provides an easy way to tell if you are thinking in the realm of the ego (not your friend) or the True Self (the place of divine connection and alignment). When you are disturbed, ask yourself these questions:

- Is this thought about gaining control over something or someone?

- Am I looking for approval in this thought?
- Is my motivation the desire for survival?

If you are answering yes to one or more of these questions, then you are in the clutches of the ego (as defined in yoga, not by Freud). Remember the ego is the opposite of the Self. Some have said that the object of many spiritual paths is to recognize the ego and to disengage it or, some say, destroy it. I prefer the notion of recognizing it, noting it, and then sending it on its way— maybe even with a little laugh. The ego hates to be laughed at.

Try asking yourself these questions and see what results. We are functioning in this world play, so guidelines are helpful. By the way, when I started doing this years ago, I was often answering "yes" to all three questions. I had previously thought I was doing pretty well in life. Why? Because my ego was answering the question. Be patient. It might take a little while to get the hang of it.

As always, do not use any of these lessons to judge or berate yourself. Not ever! Remember that you love yourself completely NOW, even if your thoughts are in disarray. They are just thoughts, after all, and not who you are, at the core of your Divine Being.

Erwin Schrodinger, who won the Nobel Prize in Physics in 1933, wrote:

"Every man's world picture is and always remains a construct of his mind and cannot be proved to have any other existence."

Lesson 45

FINDING THE GOLD
WITHIN YOURSELF

"The final mystery is oneself."
—Oscar Wilde

Isn't it odd that we are so hard on ourselves? That we, the ones who live in this body and have a pretty good idea of our history and likes and dislikes, seem to wrestle with knowing who we really are? We get all mixed up in thinking false ideas. We hook ourselves up to the definitions made by the ego and go on our not-so-merry way. We define ourselves by outward notions—things like our name, our education level, our race, our appearance, our nationality, our income, our family, our possessions, even our weight—and then wonder why happiness eludes us.

We are searching in all the wrong places. We have to peel away the layers, as one might envision the thin layers of an onion. In the *Yoga Sutras,* we refer to this as self-study. We try to honestly and actively pursue the removing of these layers so our true and Divine Self can emerge into the Light. This practice is called, in Sanskrit, *svadhyaya.* Self reflection.

SELF STUDY

Thomas Merton, an Anglo-American Catholic monk and mystic, has written:

"The first step toward finding God, who is Truth, is to discover the truth about myself."

There are many means to accomplish this task. Honestly observing our interactions with those around us is one way. Another is by pursuing the reading of spiritual texts that enlighten us as to the traits of loving kindness. For some, chanting a mantra, meditating, doing yoga poses, walking in nature, praying, helping others are effective. Showing genuine forgiveness and kindness to ourselves and others can be a form of self-study. Other people may see going to confession as useful, or following various rituals that encourage self-examination. As the external layers are removed, we are lighter and feel cleansed.

I have been in Bangkok, Thailand several times, and each time I have gone to The Temple of the Golden Buddha. I never tire of the story. I hope you will like it, too.

Over 300 years ago when then Siam was being attacked, a group of monks wanting to protect their golden Buddha that was ten feet tall and weighed at least two and a half tons, covered it with twelve inches of clay. They felt certain that it would be ignored and not taken. They were right, but, unfortunately, all the monks were slaughtered and the secret was lost. Then in the mid 1950s, the monastery that housed the statue had to be moved to another location. A crane was brought in to raise the clay Buddha, but the crane was not powerful enough as the Buddha was so heavy. The Buddha was dropped and a small part of the clay cracked. Taking a flashlight, the head monk saw something shining brightly through the crack. As he chipped away, he found what was enclosed inside—a solid gold Buddha that had been encased in clay.

This is like ourselves. We mistake ourselves to be nothing but clay. Common, ordinary clay. But we too have a golden light so brilliant and a love so eternal that we fail to see what is inside of us. But when we look with kindness and compassion, we will find the treasure and feel the elation. We then know who we truly are and this surpasses the most rudimentary concepts of happiness. It is bliss!

Some ideas:

- Look honestly at yourself. You will likely know if there are behaviors within yourself that trouble you. Are you short with some people? Are you condescending? Are you even cruel? Begin peeling, little by little, and count each change as a triumph.
- Be grateful when you can see yourself more plainly. There need be no fear. They are only thoughts. Be grateful for inner wisdom.
- Is there someone with whom to share your journey inward? Maybe within a religious context? Or a spiritual mentor? Or a trusted friend? Maybe they will want to join you in this adventure.
- Do not get lost in feeling guilt or shame. It is easy to do this. Forgiveness and compassion begin with you.
- Watch as you become lighter and happier, more authentically you.
- Be patient. It could take some time. Time does not matter. You are on the path.
- Keep saying "I love myself completely NOW," throughout the process.

August Wilson, the Pulitzer Prize winning playwright said:

*"Confront the dark parts of yourself and work to banish them
with illumination and forgiveness.
Your willingness to wrestle with your
demons will cause your angels to sing."*

It might delight Wilson to think that we are all actors in a play. The play of *maya*. That the gold at the core of our being remains the definition of who we are. Perfect and the Light of Eternal Love, that's who. Nothing has changed. It is who we have always been!

Lesson 46

WHAT HAPPENS IF YOU REALLY CONCENTRATE?

"For him who has no concentration, there is no tranquility."
—The Bhagavad Gita

How scattered we are. Most of our lives we seem to skitter from one task to another, from one plan to another, and from one thought to another. And then, before we know it, another year has passed, and we are still marking our lives by time and place, by goals met or not met, and by exterior measurements. But what is happening inside, at the core of our being? Have we spent even a small amount of time in considering what is transcendent and eternal? Have we made any progress at all in feeling rested, calm, peaceful, and tranquil? Has the idea of finding true happiness and contentedness occurred to us? What, I wonder, are we waiting for?

Dharana, the sixth of the eight limbs of the *Yoga Sutras*, offers us guidance and inspiration. It helps us to develop concentration that can change our lives.

CONCENTRATION—*DHARANA*

I am not sure how it happened to me. Many years ago, I had an experience some call *shaktipat,* a spontaneous opening into Truth and a spark of enlightenment. I didn't expect it and had little idea what it meant. Of course, I had been studying yoga and teaching for some time, but this was way beyond anything I could have anticipated. My life changed in seconds. Somehow I was spontaneously drawn to certain behavioral changes. One of them could have been identified as *dharana;* I began to focus on the mantra *Om Namah Shivaya.* The mantra was not only present during meditation. I chanted it either out loud or quietly almost every waking moment. And I continued to do this for months. If I was in a place where I could not chant it out loud, I had my *mala* (like rosary) beads I could inconspicuously move through my fingers, knowing that the mantra flowed with each touch. I was steeped in concentration, and miracles began to unfold around me. Long-held concepts like time and space began to show that they were not so fixed after all. I was shocked when I watched time slow down when I needed it to. Wow, I would think to myself with wonder, how did that happen?

Certainly, you don't have to choose something in *Sanskrit* or anything else that is not familiar to you. Not at all. You could choose to focus on an image, like a rose or a statue, or you could give concentration to a word, like peace or love or God. Whatever you choose, you must try to block out everything else. This is, in fact, a kind of precursor to a good meditation practice, but you don't have to see it that way. Just let it be, preferably in the morning before too much is happening. Make it a delineated time, say, ten minutes or more, when you give attention to nothing, nothing else. This shows you how to discipline your mind, to ward off extraneous thoughts, and creates a sense of great power. If you can hold steady during this time, you can also do it at other times. It is a reserve for when you might really need this strength.

Some say the mind is like a drunken monkey, reeling us around, flitting from limb to limb, and crazy making. But once you know how to concentrate, you are merely the observer of the monkey. The monkey might still be there, it just does not define you. I can observe myself sometimes caught in the monkey trap. But I have learned to be kind and forgiving and compassionate when this happens. I also know it is temporary and what really matters is planted deeply and unshakably within me. *Om Namah Shivaya.*

Years ago one of my students told me that her children got used to her saying or chanting *Om Namah Shivaya* as she went about her day. Saying it soothed her. At some point, she recounted, she hit a bad patch and got very upset about something going on around her. She was visibly upset, at which point her daughter ran up to her, and with insistence said, "Oh, Mama, *Om Namah Shivaya. Om Namah Shivaya.*" It was the Band-Aid to bring everything back to normal.

Some ideas:

- Think of something that will soothe you, that you can spend time focusing on for periods of time everyday. Some word or words, an object, a painting, anything will do. At first, you can experiment until you find your concentration object. Try it out.
- Once you have chosen it, choose a time, block it out, when you will do your practice of *dharana*. Then stay with it. Be patient. Trust in it.
- Don't expect an overnight miracle (though it could happen). It will likely require weeks or even months to notice pattern changes in your life.

- Return to your concentration object throughout the day. Let it be your natural tendency to go back to it, perhaps cued by something you have chosen—on every hour, whenever the phone rings, when you see something around you.

One of the most highly respected thinkers and spiritual teachers of our time is the late Ramana Maharshi. He said:

"The degree of freedom from unwanted thoughts and the degree of concentration on a single thought are the measures to gauge spiritual success."

With concentration, you will meet your True Self and abide in Love and Light.

Lesson 47

LIGHTEN UP! LAUGH!
IT'S GOOD FOR YOU!

Go ahead. Lighten up! Indulge yourself. Have a good laugh. You will be doing more to benefit yourself than you might imagine! Your body and mind will indeed feel lighter because you will be releasing happy hormones into your system. You will be increasing the strength of your immune system. The oxygen levels will be greater in both your body and your brain. You will cast out anxiety and stress, all while having a good time doing it. And you will increase the energy of light and joy and love all around you. It sounds like a pretty good deal to me.

One of my favorite yoga classes has been on this very subject of being light. In class we focus on feeling our bodies growing lighter and more free. We laugh freely throughout the class and sometimes share our favorite jokes. One of mine is this, "What did the yogi say to the hot dog vendor?" "Make me one with everything." Haha. Then the yogi gave the hot dog vendor a $20 bill. When no change was offered, the yogi said, "Hey, where's the change?" The vendor said, "Change comes from within." Hahahaha!

While on the surface it may appear that this class is a trivial thing, surely it is not. It offers important lessons about seeing ourselves as the Light itself. It helps us to not take ourselves or the world too seriously. It serves as a reminder that everything, including the goofy and wacky, is there for us as a gift of Divine Consciousness.

Lighten Up!

Any moment is the perfect moment to lighten up! I especially like this practice during autumn and winter as daylight hours diminish where I live in the Northeast United States. Some of us start to feel starved for light. Holidays arrive with the traditions of lighted candles and sparkling glitter. But it is nice to know that we, you and I, carry the Light within us all the time, and we experience it in many ways.

Swami Muktananda, a Siddha Yoga guru who has inspired many of my teachings and who seemed to take me under his wing (though he had already left his body or, as we say, he died) said this:

*"See the world as a divine play, as the light of your own soul,
and enjoy it while still laughing happily."*

I have fond memories of a video containing many clips of him laughing. It was shown at a special ceremony at an ashram celebrating Muktananda's life. The laughter on the screen was contagious. After that, and much to my surprise, it seemed that he took to manifesting some very funny objects into my yoga room, all with a lesson contained within. He taught me the value of laughing and being light.

I needed that lesson! It helped me to remember that Dr. Bernie Seigel, the author of many books about those facing life threatening diseases, always lauds the miraculous ability of laughter in the process of healing. In recent years, a new kind of yoga has emerged. It is called Laughter Yoga. It encourages childlike playfulness that results in bursts of natural laughter (who wouldn't like a return to this?). It was begun in India by a medical doctor, Madan Kataria, seeking to learn if cancer patients who laughed (in this special class he invented) would be more likely to heal. Proof was shown and today Laughter Yoga is circling the globe.

What about you? Are you weighted down with so many serious responsibilities that there is no time to laugh? Go ahead! Give yourself permission! Let's call it a prescription for good health and happiness. The doctor orders that you prioritize laughter! Here are some ideas:

- Watch a funny movie. Maybe something you have seen before or a new one. Pick one that makes you laugh out loud.
- Hang out with a friend with whom you can share some funny times, someone who makes you laugh and encourages this lightness within you. If you can't see someone in person, call them on the telephone. I have some friends who share my ludicrous and silly sense of humor and I always feel so much happier after talking with them. No one else understands our merriment, but we do.
- Choose a book of cartoons or humorous writing. I have favorites around the house. *The Far Side* still makes me laugh and a big coffee table book of cartoons of *The New Yorker* is guaranteed to evoke humor, though not the same as the sillier books I have.
- Remember moments in the past when you laughed uncontrollably. You know the kind of laughter that can't be suppressed but bubbles over. I have many to draw from.

- Check out TV programs, even old ones. We have the complete set of the Monty Python series. One look at the "silly walks" and I will be laughing.
- Seek out original and novel ways to laugh. Put it on your schedule as a priority.

Remember that it is up to you to choose your form of humor. Let it spring directly from your heart and soul. Let it sustain you. See how much lighter and happier your life will become—and how much healthier you will be, as a special side benefit. I'm not kidding!

Lesson 48

I Am Grateful.
I Am Thankful.

"If the only prayer you say in your
life is 'thank you,' that would suffice."

Meister Eckhart wrote those wise words. In their simplicity they
provide a lesson for all of us. We often lose sight of the many reasons we have to be grateful and thankful. In the United States,
the most universally celebrated holiday is Thanksgiving. While
this once-a-year day is valued and important to most of us, the
Thanksgiving Day toast is hardly enough. Every day can be
thanksgiving, even for the simplest gifts.

Being grateful and thankful increases our levels of happiness
and engenders a sense of well-being. Many writings on happiness recommend that we make a list of our blessings, write them
down, and remember them right before we go to sleep at night,
thus helping to pave the way for a peaceful sleep. I find that listing my reasons to be grateful helps me to remember the big and
little reasons I have to be thankful. They may include having
a comfortable bed for sleeping. Having kind and loving friends.
Having the means to enjoy nutritious food and have warmth in

the cold winter months. Enjoying an ice cream sundae. Having good health. You can see where I am going and can take it from there. You can also see how easy it is. And there is a surprise. A miracle surrounds this act of gratitude. Even on your darkest day, in the midst of sadness or grief, you will experience a lifting, and you can make contact with the light within you.

THANKFULNESS

Before I began writing *The 52*, I blogged on many subjects. This is the one I wrote on gratitude. I like it so much I decided to include it again.

Instead of focusing on what we don't have, on the negatives, on the injustices, on the minutia of aggravations that go on, feeling gratitude is for many of us another way to think. We can easily find criticism in our everyday life—with the surly driver, the craziness of the political scene, the screaming and disconcerting headlines. That is a slam dunk! Wallow in it if it you must, but don't forget what is really important. You have a choice!

Irving Berlin wrote a song that Bing Crosby performed in the film, *White Christmas*. It is called "Count Your Blessings (Instead of Sheep)" and reminds us that instead of being worried and unable to sleep at night, you can always count your blessings. It also suggests that "if your bankroll is getting small," you might instead remember when "you had none at all." It is likely that generations of young people have never heard the song, but this does not make the words any less valid. They speak of a sleepy time practice that can bring happiness to the heart. Why not fall asleep counting your blessings? Couldn't we all use a little of that?

Some ways to remember gratitude:

- Make it a nightly practice to either write down or recite to yourself five reasons you have for being grateful.
- Ask a friend to join you in remembering thankfulness. Discuss it with someone. Share the joy.
- Send a note, text, email to someone and tell them you appreciate them and why.
- Call someone on the phone and do the same thing.
- Thank someone for their help or service. It could be the dry cleaner or person who delivers the mail or the one checking you out of the grocery store. Anyone. Spread the joy and gratitude.
- Think of someone you love who touched your life in a deep way. Perhaps someone who has left this plane and died. You can thank them too. Don't worry. They will hear you, whether you believe this or not.
- Include yourself. Be grateful for the person you are who has done a kindness for another. Applaud yourself simply for being you.
- And there is another to thank. Choose the name you like—God, the Divine, Supreme Consciousness, Allah, the Buddha, Jesus, Shiva. A small thank you is a very big thing.

Many years ago, I learned an unexpected lesson about gratitude when my husband and I traveled to East Africa. As we wandered through a small village near Arusha, Tanzania, we had the good fortune to make the acquaintance of a young man and father who resided in one of the tiny enclaves of mud huts. He spoke English, took us to his home, and in the course of a few hours, became someone we would call a friend. In this, one of our first journeys into a Third World country, we felt determined to help him. After returning home, we sent simple gifts to him and his children. Practical items for school, books, medications, cash hidden in places where he would find it. We soon learned some hard lessons. Some of the packages were scrutinized or stolen. To our horror, he was accosted and beaten, his home ransacked in search of special items. In time, we heard no more from him. We were deeply saddened and worried that our naive generosity had led to misfortune. Why would I tell this story now? Because I am grateful to be in a country where this is much less likely to happen. Because I never forget to be thankful for the freedoms we so blithely enjoy. Because I have a long list of thank you's and, in many places in the world, what I take for granted is not so possible. I still wonder what happened to that bright and hopeful young man.

The playwright, Thornton Wilder, said this:

"We can only be said to be alive in those moments when our hearts are conscious of our treasures."

What are your treasures? What makes you thankful? Try counting your blessings. You may be surprised at the richness of your life, just as it is right now.

Lesson 49

THE COURAGE TO SURRENDER

*"Surrender is the faith that the
power of Love can accomplish anything
even when you cannot foresee the outcome."*
—Deepak Chopra

The idea of surrender is not easy for many of us. We function in the belief that we must be in control at all times. We make the false assumption that surrender implies weakness and passivity. We have grown so attached to this incorrect notion that our egos (which IS us to many of us) is the only hope. So we place our trust, not in the all-powerful Divine that is the eternal us (the Self) at the core of our being, and hook our belief to the ever-changing, never reliable ego. Such is the pity.

If only we had the courage to surrender! And, trust in this, not only do you have the courage, it is, in fact, the place of the greatest reliability. Letting go is the starting point where a peaceful life begins. We might call it trust in God or any other concept you hold that expresses to you Eternal Light and Love.

Surrender

"Thy will be done." Years ago, Dr. Larry Dossey wrote about the power of prayer in several books including *Healing Words.* His findings at the time were considered groundbreaking. He cited many studies that showed that some kind of "non-local" thinking or prayer could be transferred out into the energy fields where tangible results were corroborated. When people said "My thoughts and prayers are with you," they might not have known how much power they were conveying. Prayers DO make a difference, yet some are more powerful than others. The "God as Santa Claus" prayers, (those which gave out a list of what was wanted, like a child's list to Santa at Christmas) could not match those that implied surrender. The most powerful prayer of all is "Thy will be done." Surrender and trust!

As most religions speak of surrender, so, too, does yoga. With *The 52,* I have sought to share the brilliance of the *Yoga Sutras* as a powerful guideline for all of us. The wisdom transcends religion *per se,* and can be effectively embraced by all, atheists and those of any belief system.

Throughout this course we have reviewed the first two rungs or limbs of Eight Limbed Yoga. Within the *Niyamas* (ethical guidelines and inner practices), comes the final lesson of surrender. It is called, in Sanskrit, *Ishvara Pranidhana,* and shows us how surrender is a virtue and a significant sacred shift that changes our lives. This shift has the power to reunite us with the True Self, the eternal being that defines us. It can effectively empty the ego of its influences and align us with Universal Consciousness.

All this power! But this doesn't mean it is an easy lesson for many of us to learn. It has been one of my biggest challenges. And I had to learn it over and over again. It took dire circumstances to wrestle me free of the ego's powerful force and the misery I was experiencing.

Several years ago, my elderly mother moved into our home. She was 95 years old at the time, had an active and lucid mind, but was faced with several medical conditions that limited her mobility. I jumped to meet the challenges but I underestimated totally what it would take. Being a full-time caregiver and juggling work was more than I could handle, even though I still taught yoga classes and meditated everyday. I was not about to surrender and accept how hard it was. Instead, I fought ever more to keep her healthy and safe while I was falling apart physically, mentally, and financially. And then we ran out of options. She was over 98 years old, her body was worn out and she was too tired to go on. We were told to call on hospice. Even then, I held out hope that she would pull through. What was I thinking? But the day came when it was clear to all of us, my mother, my husband and me, that we had no control over any of this. We could not change anything. We could only surrender and wait. That's when the miracles began in earnest. We let go, and it became a sacred sharing for all three of us. We surrendered at last. Her parting became a sacred passing, full of Love and Light.

Of course I know that learning to surrender does not have to be under such sad and dramatic circumstances. But now I can see when I am resistant and when surrender is the path to take. My favorite Sufi poet, Rumi has written:

"They are the chosen ones who have surrendered."

A few ideas that might help:
- When you've programmed your day and will never finish all your tasks, think about letting some of them go. What's the big deal? Who is judging anyway?

- When you know that you are feeling fatigue, give yourself a break. Go within for a while, take some refreshing cleansing breathes. Have a cup of tea. Or even take a little nap.
- Have you ever been at the airport and your flight is delayed or cancelled? I used to rant. Now I check out my options and try to "go with the flow." I feel much better this way.
- Say to yourself, "Relax!" While there was a time when saying it was anathema to me, I can now easily say, "Thy will be done."

"If you surrender completely to the moments as they pass, you live more richly those moments."
—Anne Morrow Lindburgh

Go ahead. Take the leap. Let go. Some call it, "let go and let God handle it." Let the winds of surrender carry you higher and higher. Now you will soar like an eagle! Or maybe even like an angel!

Lesson 50

THE WAY TO THE LIGHT.
IT'S WITH YOU ALL THE TIME

Wouldn't you like to have an easy way to measure your thinking and your health? Something that travels with you like a
personal physician? What you are looking for is already there,
acting like your own private measuring device. It is the doctor
at your side. Through the hustles and bustles of your life, all
you have to do is stop for a few seconds and get a reading. A
handy-dandy guide.

Good news! You have it with you all the time. It has been there
ever since you were born. It travels with you through thick and
thin. It is there when you are sleeping and when you are awake.
It is one of the most powerful tools for transformation, for remembering the Light and Love within you, for placing your
entire life in balance. It cuts through stress and negative thinking. All you have to do is remember to work with it. And, just
in case you are not inclined to spiritual or God thinking, it will
never fail you. What could it be?

It is the breath. It is what you are doing right now. Have you
learned to pay attention to it? Are you conscious of it? You don't

need to tie a ring around your finger to remind you of spiritual practices or aphorisms. Your breath is there all the time, just waiting to be noticed and used to help you.

When I began *The 52*, I promised simple lessons that could guide you to a lighter and happier and more loving life. As the lessons wind down, it is important to return to one that everyone can use. Everyone! You are breathing right now, aren't you?

LET YOUR BREATH GUIDE YOU TO THE LIGHT.

"If you can control your breath, you can control your life."

Those were the words I heard when I began studying the breath, under the guidance of medical doctors, psychologists, and a swami—all of whom had collaborated on a book called *The Science of Breath*. They were renowned for their knowledge of the subject of breathing. Nonetheless, I didn't really believe what they said; it was too far-fetched for me then. You may not believe me as I restate it now, but trust me, it is a true statement.

Why is the breath so important? For starters, if you are not breathing, you are not alive. It is why we say things like "when he took his last breath." You need oxygen to live, but that is simple stuff. We all know that, I think.

We yogis also believe that the subtle energy called *prana* is carried on the breath. It is a profound energy source that enlivens our bodies on more than a physical level. It streams through the thousands of *nadis* (numbering at anywhere from 72,000 to 350,000) and into the ever-swirling *chakras*, the primary subtle energy centers generally associated with their locations all along the spinal column. These *nadis* and *chakras* exist in what we call the "subtle body", not the physical body. The energy of *prana* purifies and balances us.

But this is more about how you breathe and what you associate with the breath. When you calm your breath, you calm your body and your mind. If the breath is shallow, fast, tense, and agitated, it reflects on your mood and health.

Here are some ideas to carry with you all the time:

- Right now! How are you breathing? Try to pay attention for half a minute or so. Let the breath move into your belly, thus creating a deeper breath. Keep it going. Don't pause and hold your breath. Keep it going through your nose, not exhaling through the mouth.
- Pay attention to the quality of the breath. If it is ragged and jagged, consciously try to smooth it out. Smooth in and smooth out.
- Imagine that every breath carries healing and light within it. Inhale light. Exhale darkness.
- Think of the breath flowing through every cell of your body, cleansing, purifying, and bringing peace to all organs and tissues.
- If you have areas of tension or pain in your body, empower your breath to heal. Healing energy into the body, pain or anxiety flowing out as you exhale.
- Give your breath words to accompany it. Choose an affirmation or sounds. "I love myself completely NOW." "I feel peace and calm throughout my body and mind." You choose what you like.

Trust me. Every one of these practices will work, if you sincerely try. In time, you will be able to monitor your condition simply by paying attention to the breath. This is a simple skill that will bring great change into your life. It doesn't require anyone else or extensive training or a trip to the therapist.

How about it? Isn't it time to learn to control your breath and therefore, control your life?

Lesson 51

STOP SEARCHING.
YOU ARE THE DESTINATION

God is a great underground river that
no one can dam up and no one can stop.
—Meister Eckhart

We search and search. We study and pray. We read books and
scriptures. We meditate. We question. We doubt. We avoid and
negate. We humans are not passive about God, even when we
actively deny the existence of some "thing" called God or the
Infinite or the Source or the Creator. Most of the greatest
minds in the world—from many disciplines including science
and philosophy—have pondered the quintessential questions
about God. Are we searching for meaning to our own existence, for something more than the mundane birth to death
and day-to-day aspects of our life? And for those of us who
are seekers on the spiritual path, it may seem surprising to
finally come to the conclusion that we, ourselves, turn out to
be the destination we seek. That all we had to do was knock
on the door and the Light would emerge from within us. Not
from outside.

Where Is God?

"What we seek is seeking us."

So spoke the great Sufi poet/saint, Rumi. He got it. So did Jesus. He said in Luke 17:21 (KJV):

"Neither shall they say, Lo here! or lo there! for, behold, the kingdom of God is within you."

Yes! Within you right now, just where God has always been. Not in some throne up in the sky, sending out judgments that reflect only our own ego needs about judging and approval and sin and death. After years of separating myself from a God belief that was based on a child's view of God, I now see only the Eternal Light of Divine Love springing from the one I care to call God.

It does not matter whether or not you agree with me. I don't seek to argue the logic of it. For years, I postured and felt smug in my arguments against God. Now my belief system has left logic behind a long time ago. Why? Because I had the "experience" of God, and the joy was so immense, there was no turning back. It is odd that it does not matter what you believe. The Divine is within all of us, no matter who we are, whatever our religion or lack of it. That is how immeasurable that Love is.

Swami Vivekananada wrote:

*"The moment I have realized God
sitting in the temple of every human body,
the moment I stand before every
human being and see God in him—
that moment I am free from bondage, everything that binds
vanishes, and I am free."*

For those of us who wish to explore and look inward, this becomes both a great freedom and a change that alters our perception of the world. How can we look upon another, seeing God's Light equally in them, and still practice violence and prejudice and hatred? They are us! And we are all equal in this great Love from God.

We are not some unworthy, soiled piece of cloth. The expectation of all true spiritual paths is that we transform our thinking, that we abandon notions that we are unforgiving and lacking and not the embodiment of love. Most of us have wallowed in the pains of our own constructed world, not realizing that it is nothing more than a play, and, we, as actors in this play, still sit in the audience and extend love to our own false identity as the player.

As *The 52* draws to a close, I believe that the suggestions in this lesson are among the most valued of all I have learned over twenty-five years of study, teaching, mystical experiences, and communion with the Divine. While it took a little while for me to completely embrace and understand the relevance of what I write here, I can only say that peace is ever more present and fear has diminished. This can be true for you, too.

> *"Out beyond the ideas of wrong-doing*
> *and right-doing, there is a field.*
> *I'll meet you there."*
> —Rumi

Shall we make it a date? I will look forward to meeting you there.

Lesson 52

AND FINALLY AND ONLY—LOVE

"Love surrounds you.
Of this be sure.
You do not walk alone."

These words, from *A Course in Miracles,* form the essence of
The 52. It is first, last, and always, the only and most important
Truth to know and believe. Recognize it at the core of your being. It is the path to true freedom. Love destroys fear and the
insidious messages of the ego, which you may have mistakenly
taken to be the truth. But hatred, judgment, anger, and hos-
tility have no power where Love resides. The darkness has no
power over the Light. It never has and never will.

Don't be mistaken, this is not some trivial, maudlin, senti-
mental kind of love—the kind you might find in typical movies
and songs and romance novels. It is beyond physical love and
that which is between individuals, though this kind of love
carries a seed of Divine Love. This is BIG, BOLD LOVE. It is
not dependent on fluctuations in temperament or on the way

the world is evolving or on another person. It does not wax and wane. It is only about you and the Divine Consciousness within you.

LOVE YOURSELF NOW

The image of the blue butterfly soaring toward the light conveys what *The 52* is meant to represent. It reflects how we, as humans, seek to find freedom and peace and the ability to feel and express love. Sometimes we are not aware of this longing, but, nonetheless, it is there. The butterfly transforms itself, from the caterpillar that crawls on the earth, to a beautiful creature with wings outspread, flying in freedom. All of us, no matter how much we think we are tied to the earth, have the capacity and wisdom to take flight. We can experience metamorphosis, just like the butterfly. Our wings may be folded now inside a cocoon, waiting. But then Love will split the cocoon and we will all fly free into the Light of Eternal and Divine Love. All of us! No one is left behind!

Once this happens—when you have even a glimpse of this Light—you will never be the same again. You will know in the depth of your heart who and what you are. You will recognize that you are not alone in this journey. This is my purpose in writing. To tell you this and that I am with you as a fellow traveler. Many others are with you. Infinite souls stand with you. We will all find each other, just as you have found this writing.

In the *Chandogya Upanishad,* an ancient book of spiritual writings from India, it is written:

> *"There is a light that shines beyond all*
> *things on earth, beyond us all, beyond the heavens,*
> *beyond the highest, the very highest heavens.*
> *This is the light that shines in our heart."*

It isn't out there, somewhere. It isn't beyond your grasp. It doesn't depend on who you are, your good deeds, your history, and your worthiness. It is your birthright, given to you for all time. It was there before you took birth. It will be there when you take your last breath and depart this plane. It is eternal. And it is present in this very moment, as you read these words. Even if you and your ego doubt it, Divine Love and Consciousness do not. I believe in it now to the core of my being, even though there was a time when I would have laughed at the notion. Others have found the same Truth and many may have expressed it with greater influence or more wisely, yet I believe that it is my purpose to share it. It was illuminated to me as the greatest gift of my life. This gift is meant to be shared.

So, here I stand, firmly grounded and steadfast and soaring with this Truth. You are Love. Love is you. Love is in everything you hear, see, taste, touch and smell. Love is ever-present and a present to you. To deny this is tantamount to denying yourself and all that is.

"I love myself completely NOW." This was the affirmation of the first lesson of *The 52*. And so it is also the last. If you have embraced this, repeated it over and over no matter the circumstances, you will in fact, BE—lighter and happier and more in touch with Divine Love than you were when you began. I promised that if you followed the course, you would be a lighter and happier and more loving you in 52 lessons and 52 weeks. That you would discover the True You. I hope that you have.

These writings and my beliefs have been non-denominational and have been planted in the spiritual belief systems of all faiths, tribes, and philosophies, all of which, at the core, share Love as the common and most important center of teaching and knowing. Here, from the Holy Bible, is a favorite of mine.

From I Corinthians 13:

"Love bears all things, believes all things, endures all things. Love never ends."

Believe in Love. Love never ends. Not ever!

Love is the TRUE YOU!

The After Words

Lesson 52 is complete. Just as the 52 lessons began with Love, so they ended. Love is the ultimate spiritual practice. It holds everything within it. My heart has felt opened and filled with Love in writing each word.

If you are so inclined, I would value your feedback. Some of you would like a means of communicating with others who are reading *The 52*. I would also like to know more about you. In addition to my many readers across the U.S., *The 52*, as a blog, developed a large following in several other countries including Ireland, China, The Netherlands, and Russia.

When I began writing *The 52* as a blog, I did so rather spontaneously (and perhaps, audaciously.) I decided to put into print the many teachings I have shared with my students and learned, both by study and reading and through mystical experiences, from many sources on my own spiritual journey. These have brought together the classic teachings of yoga and the mystical branches of many religions. The lessons have been informed by the teachings of Jesus, the Buddha, Rumi and other Sufi masters, native and aboriginal traditions, Judaic mystical writings, ancient Hindu texts and other forms of inspired spiritual lessons. While certain themes have repeated themselves, I have sought to give bullet point suggestions for you to put into practice those ideas and to offer a multitude of guidelines. Believing that all paths lead ultimately to the great Source, to the Light of Eternal and Divine Love, to Truth, to freedom, to God, each reader could choose what most resonated with them.

Years ago, I subscribed to a course provided by the Siddha lineage of yoga. At the time it was, called "The Siddha Yoga Correspondence Course" and was authored by Ram at the request of his *guru,* Muktananda. In the very first lesson, I recall reading that it would contain everything we needed to know; all subsequent lessons would be different approaches to the same theme. The lessons were surprisingly simple (as I have tried to make *The 52* simple). The course requested only that the reader repeat reading the same two lessons throughout the month, reading the words and imbibing the energy, even if the words made no particular sense. Just being present to the Divine Energy therein would be enough. And it was!

Later I began the daily lessons of *A Course in Miracles.* I have since read every word of the text and information for teachers and have repeated the workbook section more than once. Repeated reading has brought more and more spiritual benefit and insight. And finally, after being asked to do so on multiple occasions, I began Study Groups for *A Course in Miracles,* called

"Into the Light of Miracles." It is such a pleasure to share the words of the Course which I hold so dear and which informs my writing.

I hope that *The 52* bears repeating and that your depth of understanding will increase with time.

I have long felt that whatever knowledge I have been given is an entrusted gift. It has been made vivid and plain that it is my purpose to share these words of Divine Love.

And now—a request. The opportunity to change people's lives, to let them experience a lighter, happier life, and to recognize that they are Divine Love will increase exponentially when this message is shared. If *The 52* has been of benefit to you, I ask that you share it with others. My one purpose in writing these words has been to be of service and to help others. Won't you join me on this journey? I will be most grateful to you.

I thank you for your kindnesses and encouragement as I offered these sincere words from my heart. My heart bonds with yours as we see that all of us are, indeed, one. You are the Light of Eternal and Divine Love.

> *"Maybe you should know yourself for just one moment.*
> *Maybe you should glimpse your most beautiful face.*
> *Maybe you should sleep less deeply in your house of clay.*
> *Maybe you should move into the house of joy,*
> *and shine in every crevice.*
> *Maybe you are the bearer of hidden treasure.*
> *Maybe you always have been."*
> —Rumi

I think you already ARE!

ACKNOWLEDGEMENTS

Many have influenced my life, work and teachings. For those who brought knowledge and light into the spiritual writings I have studied, I am forever grateful.

To Jerry Eichengreen, whose yoga classes inspired me to become a yoga teacher.

To Gretchen Yates Lum, who has been a beloved spiritual sister and who sought me out so that I could meet her two gurus whose energy transformed my life.

To Linda Rowley Blue, my longtime friend and traveling companion, whose laughter, good humor, and spiritual insights have enriched my life.

To Berit Stanton, whom I met and knew instantly we were bonded in Divine Love.

To Henry Grayson PhD, whose depth of wisdom on many levels, as a therapist, a friend, and with whom I studied his original approaches to energy healing.

To Timothy Rowe MD, who helped me stay steady on the course with his unwavering kindness and good counsel and who helped me see that my teachings were being guided to expand.

To Swami Gurumayi Chidvalasananda and to Swami Muktananda for bringing about an awakening that changed my life forever and whose presence has been manifest ever after.

To Swami Rama and the Himalayan Institute where I did my first serious yoga work and became a certified teacher.

To all those who brought to life *A Course in Miracles,* to Jesus (the Christ) and the miracles we know. And to all who study and teach this course.

To the mystical poet, Rumi, whose words became beacons to me and who (much to my surprise) jolted me with the power of his love.

To Coleman Barks, who, with his translations of Rumi's poetry, brought the joy and understanding to his words.

To Patanjali for the immense knowledge of the *Yoga Sutras,* which first made clear that I was more than "Deanne."

To Dr. David Hawkins whose books I devoured for their wisdom and truth.

To Marlo Thomas, who has always championed women and, whose example that women of any age can set new goals, inspired my work.

To Constance Vincent, an author and one who supported this writing from the very beginning.

To all teachers and authors of books that opened my eyes further.

To all my students who entered my life and became teachers for me as well.

To my friends, too numerous to mention lest I also forget one, who have supported me throughout this spiritually evolving period of my life and who stood by me even as I often struggled.

To Martha Rhodes, an author and excellent guide and editor in shepherding this book to fruition. I am eternally grateful.

To my brother, Bill Yek, and sister-in-law, Judy Rengert, whose kindness and good counsel I trust implicitly.

To my father who left us too soon and my mother whose company I had the privilege to enjoy into her late nineties. To both of my parents for allowing enough freedom for me to take chances of all kinds, and, however these unfolded, being there no matter what.

To my husband, Richard, who has been my partner through change and challenge, in all times, who took seriously my spiritual pursuits, and whose own wisdom would indicate that he may know more about these teachings than I.

Gloria in Excelsius Deo!

Author Biography

Deanne Mincer's teaching is grounded in her steadfast belief that each of us is a being of eternal light and divine love and that we can all come to know this truth in this lifetime.

She has taught yoga and spiritual practices for more than twenty-five years. She is an enthusiastic, joyous and light-hearted conveyor of the messages she feels have been imparted to her. Deanne's extensive study brings together the combined wisdom of classic yoga texts, such as the *Yoga Sutras,* the visionary words of *A Course in Miracles,* and the revelations of the poetry of Rumi. Many mystical experiences have informed her work, brought about by enlightened teachers, both living and in spirit.

In her efforts to help us learn the consciousness of divine love, she has collaborated with Sacred Acoustics in producing *Divine Love: A Unique Yoga Nidra Experience.* This is the joining of the powerful guidance of "sleeping yoga" with the profound brain entrainment sounds and tones of Sacred Acoustics. Deanne has traveled to spiritual sites worldwide which greatly influenced her writing and teaching.

Deanne also co-authored, with her husband, Richard Mincer, *The Talk Show Book.* She is a graduate of the University of Michigan. They live in a quintessential New England town in Connecticut.

For more information or contact, please go to:

www.deannemincer.com

http://www.facebook.com/LightofEternalLove

http://www.facebook.com/deanne.mincer

http://www.twitter/DeanneMincer.

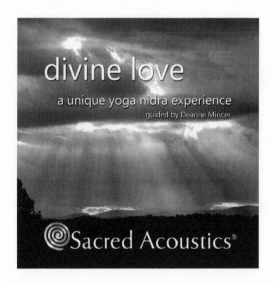

Made in the USA
Middletown, DE
11 February 2015